GRAPHIC SCIENCE BIOGRAPHIES

ADA LOVELACE AND THE START OF COMPUTERS

JORDI BAYARRI

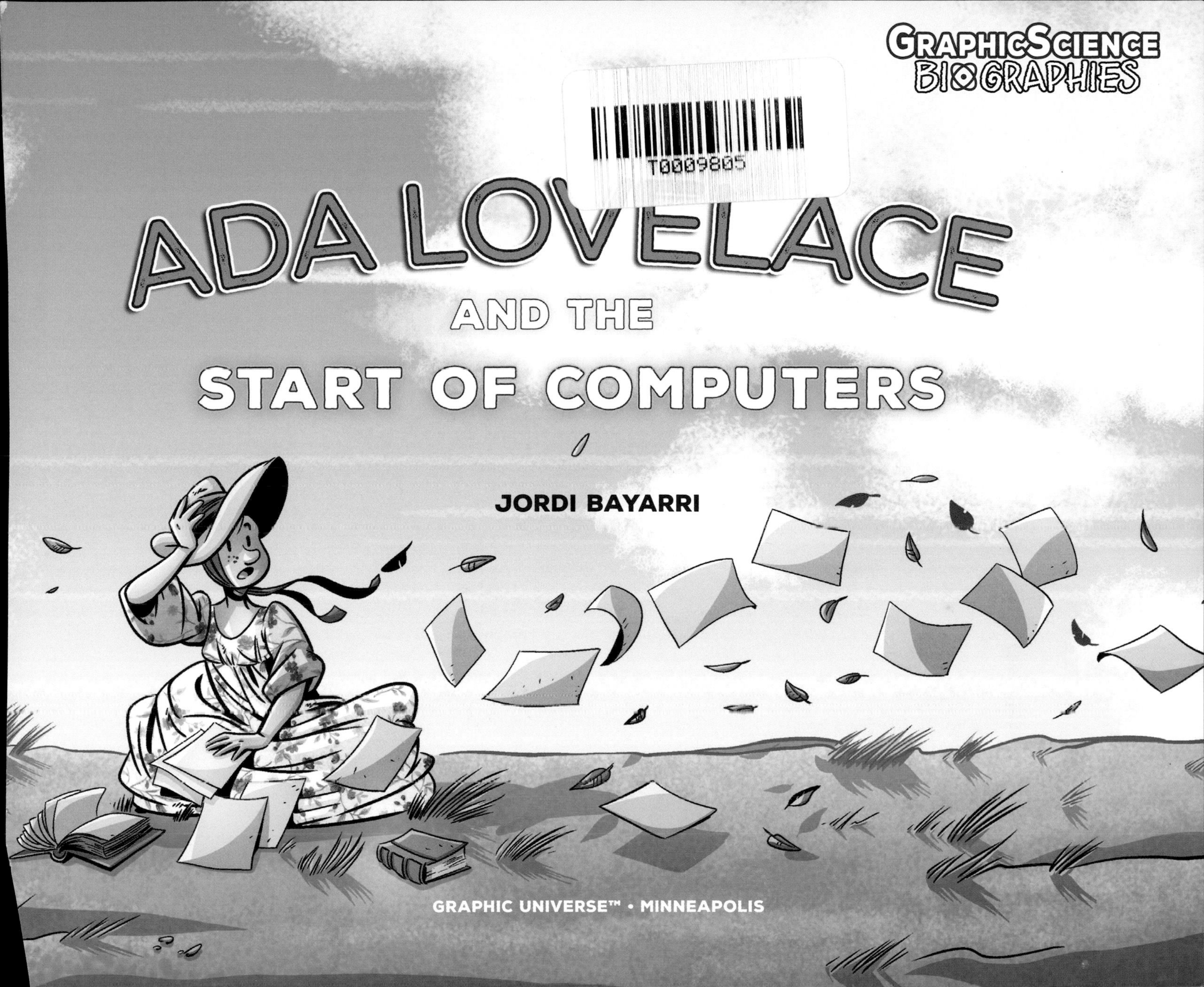

GRAPHIC UNIVERSE™ • MINNEAPOLIS

Story and art by Jordi Bayarri
Historical and scientific consultation by Dr. Tayra M. C. Lanuza-Navarro, PhD in History of Science
Translation by Sofia Huitron Martinez
Coloring by Dani Seijas
Coloring assistance by Javier Moreno
Technical assistance by Enrique Ramos Peinado

First American edition published in 2023 by Graphic Universe™
Graphic Universe™ is a trademark of Lerner Publishing Group, Inc.

Graphic Universe™
An imprint of Lerner Publishing Group, Inc.
241 First Avenue North
Minneapolis, MN 55401 USA

For reading levels and more information, look up this title at www.lernerbooks.com.

Image credit: Page 37: Ada Lovelace watercolor portrait, circa 1840. Courtesy of Science Museum Group/Wikipedia Commons (PD).

Main body text set in CCDaveGibbonsLower.
Typeface provided by Comicraft.

Library of Congress Cataloging-in-Publication Data

Names: Bayarri, Jordi, 1972– author, illustrator. | Huitrón Martínez, Sofía, translator.
Title: Ada Lovelace and the start of computers / story and art by Jordi Bayarri ; translation by Sofia Huitron Martinez
Other titles: Ada Lovelace, la encantadora de números. English
Description: First American edition. | Minneapolis : Graphic Universe, 2023. | Series: Graphic science biographies | "Ada Lovelace, la encantadora de números © by Colección Científicos; Copyright © 2019 by Jordi Bayarri." | Includes bibliographical references and index. | Audience: Ages 10–14 | Audience: Grades 4–6 | Summary: "Ada Lovelace turned her powerful imagination into a vision of the future, predicting the impact of computers on human life. Her work spread awareness of what an early computer could do"– Provided by publisher.
Identifiers: LCCN 2022008641 (print) | LCCN 2022008642 (ebook) | ISBN 9781728442914 (library binding) | ISBN 9781728478265 (paperback) | ISBN 9781728480572 (ebook)
Subjects: LCSH: Lovelace, Ada King, Countess of, 1815–1852—Juvenile literature. | Women mathematicians—Great Britain—Biography—Juvenile literature. | Women computer programmers—Great Britain—Biography—Juvenile literature. | Mathematicians—Great Britain—Biography—Juvenile literature. | Computer programmers—Great Britain—Biography—Juvenile literature. | Lovelace, Ada King, Countess of, 1815–1852—Juvenile literature. | Women mathematicians—Great Britain—Biography—Comic books, strips, etc. | Women computer programmers—Great Britain—Biography—Comic books, strips, etc. | Mathematicians—Great Britain—Biography—Comic books, strips, etc. | Computer programmers—Great Britain—Biography—Comic books, strips, etc.
Classification: LCC QA29.L72 B39 2023 (print) | LCC QA29.L72 (ebook) | DDC 510.92 [B]—dc23/eng/20220330

LC record available at https://lccn.loc.gov/2022008641
LC ebook record available at https://lccn.loc.gov/2022008642

Manufactured in the United States of America
1-50116-49806-6/8/2022

CONTENTS

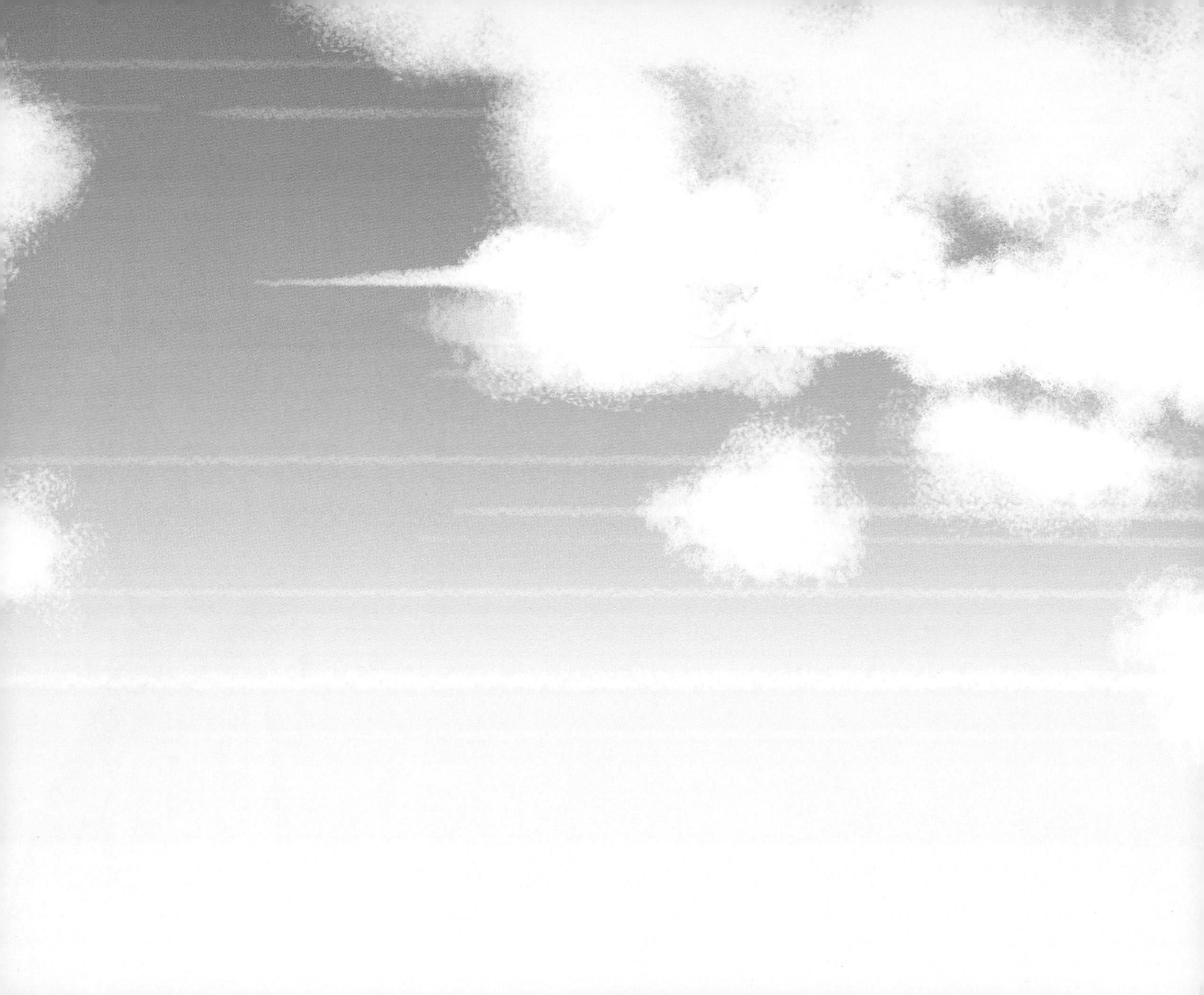

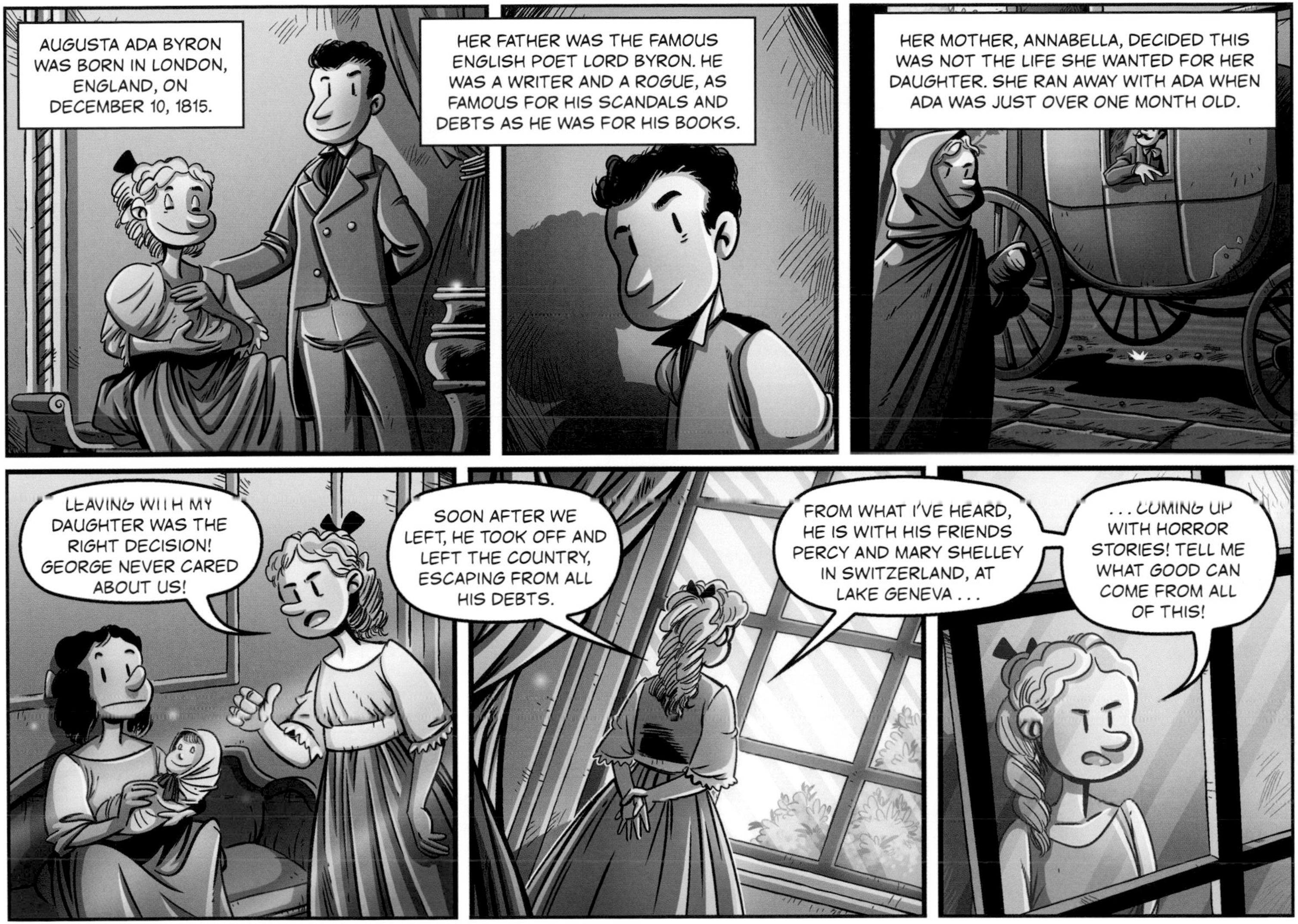
AUGUSTA ADA BYRON WAS BORN IN LONDON, ENGLAND, ON DECEMBER 10, 1815.
HER FATHER WAS THE FAMOUS ENGLISH POET LORD BYRON. HE WAS A WRITER AND A ROGUE, AS FAMOUS FOR HIS SCANDALS AND DEBTS AS HE WAS FOR HIS BOOKS.
HER MOTHER, ANNABELLA, DECIDED THIS WAS NOT THE LIFE SHE WANTED FOR HER DAUGHTER. SHE RAN AWAY WITH ADA WHEN ADA WAS JUST OVER ONE MONTH OLD.
LEAVING WITH MY DAUGHTER WAS THE RIGHT DECISION! GEORGE NEVER CARED ABOUT US!
SOON AFTER WE LEFT, HE TOOK OFF AND LEFT THE COUNTRY, ESCAPING FROM ALL HIS DEBTS.
FROM WHAT I'VE HEARD, HE IS WITH HIS FRIENDS PERCY AND MARY SHELLEY IN SWITZERLAND, AT LAKE GENEVA . . .
. . . COMING UP WITH HORROR STORIES! TELL ME WHAT GOOD CAN COME FROM ALL OF THIS!

BUT I WILL MAKE SURE ADA DOESN'T FOLLOW HER FATHER'S FOOTSTEPS.

SHE WILL STUDY MATHEMATICS, LIKE ME.

"SHE WILL GET THE BEST EDUCATION, WITH CLASSES AND A STRICT SCHEDULE."

AND NOW, LET'S PRACTICE MULTIPLICATION . . .

WATCH YOUR TONGUE! LADIES DON'T STICK THEIR TONGUES OUT!

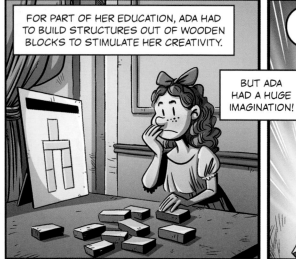

FOR PART OF HER EDUCATION, ADA HAD TO BUILD STRUCTURES OUT OF WOODEN BLOCKS TO STIMULATE HER CREATIVITY.

BUT ADA HAD A HUGE IMAGINATION!

I GOT IT!

BUT . . . THAT IS NOT THE SHAPE YOU WERE SUPPOSED TO MAKE.

I KNOW, BUT I LIKE MINE BETTER!

WHAT ARE YOU DOING?

HAVE YOU FINISHED YOUR HOMEWORK?

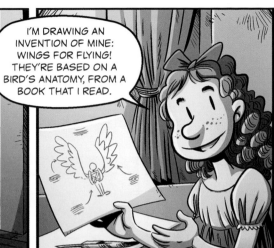

I'M DRAWING AN INVENTION OF MINE: WINGS FOR FLYING! THEY'RE BASED ON A BIRD'S ANATOMY, FROM A BOOK THAT I READ.

WINGS . . . FOR PEOPLE?

AND IT ISN'T MY ONLY FLYING DEVICE! I ALSO DESIGNED A FLYING HORSE, WITH WINGS POWERED BY STEAM!

LOOK!

YOU SHOULD BE WORKING ON YOUR STUDIES!

FLYING MACHINES? THAT'S ABSURD!

YOU'LL SEE! WHEN I GROW UP, I'LL BE AN EXPERT IN "FLYOLOGY"!

HELLO, MRS. PUFF! HAVE YOU COME TO SEE MY DRAWINGS?

MEOW!

LOOK! IT'S A MAP OF THE STARS.

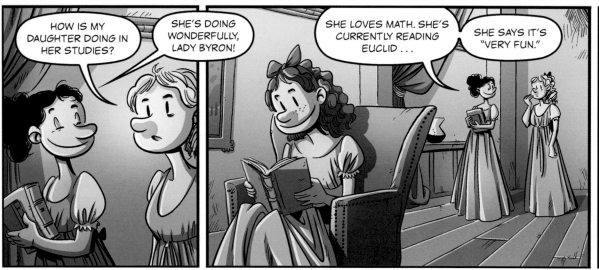

HOW IS MY DAUGHTER DOING IN HER STUDIES?

SHE'S DOING WONDERFULLY, LADY BYRON!

SHE LOVES MATH. SHE'S CURRENTLY READING EUCLID . . .

SHE SAYS IT'S "VERY FUN."

MAYBE THIS IS NOT ENOUGH. ADA NEEDS A MORE COMPLETE EDUCATION!

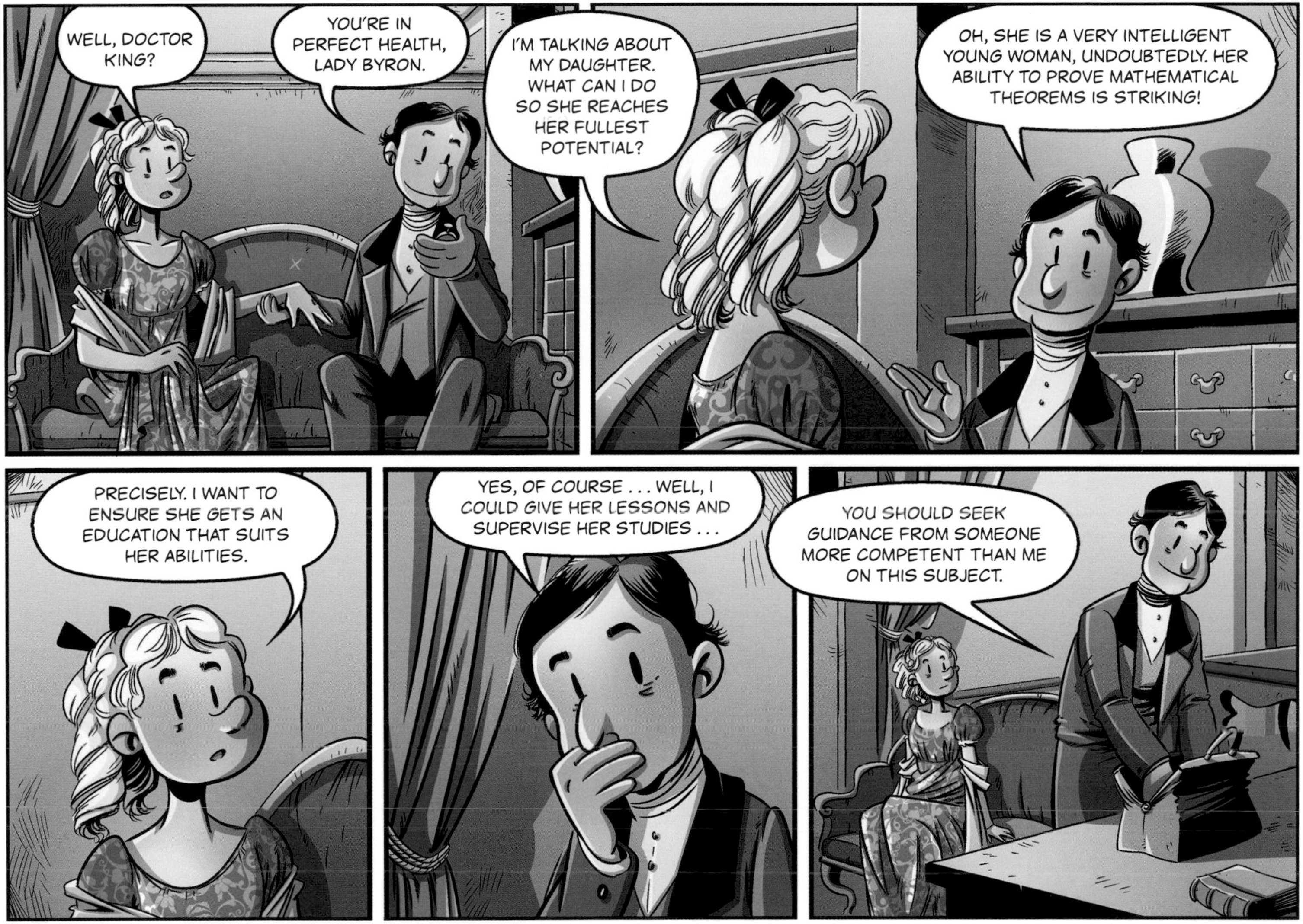
WELL, DOCTOR KING?
YOU'RE IN PERFECT HEALTH, LADY BYRON.
I'M TALKING ABOUT MY DAUGHTER. WHAT CAN I DO SO SHE REACHES HER FULLEST POTENTIAL?
OH, SHE IS A VERY INTELLIGENT YOUNG WOMAN, UNDOUBTEDLY. HER ABILITY TO PROVE MATHEMATICAL THEOREMS IS STRIKING!
PRECISELY. I WANT TO ENSURE SHE GETS AN EDUCATION THAT SUITS HER ABILITIES.
YES, OF COURSE . . . WELL, I COULD GIVE HER LESSONS AND SUPERVISE HER STUDIES . . .
YOU SHOULD SEEK GUIDANCE FROM SOMEONE MORE COMPETENT THAN ME ON THIS SUBJECT.

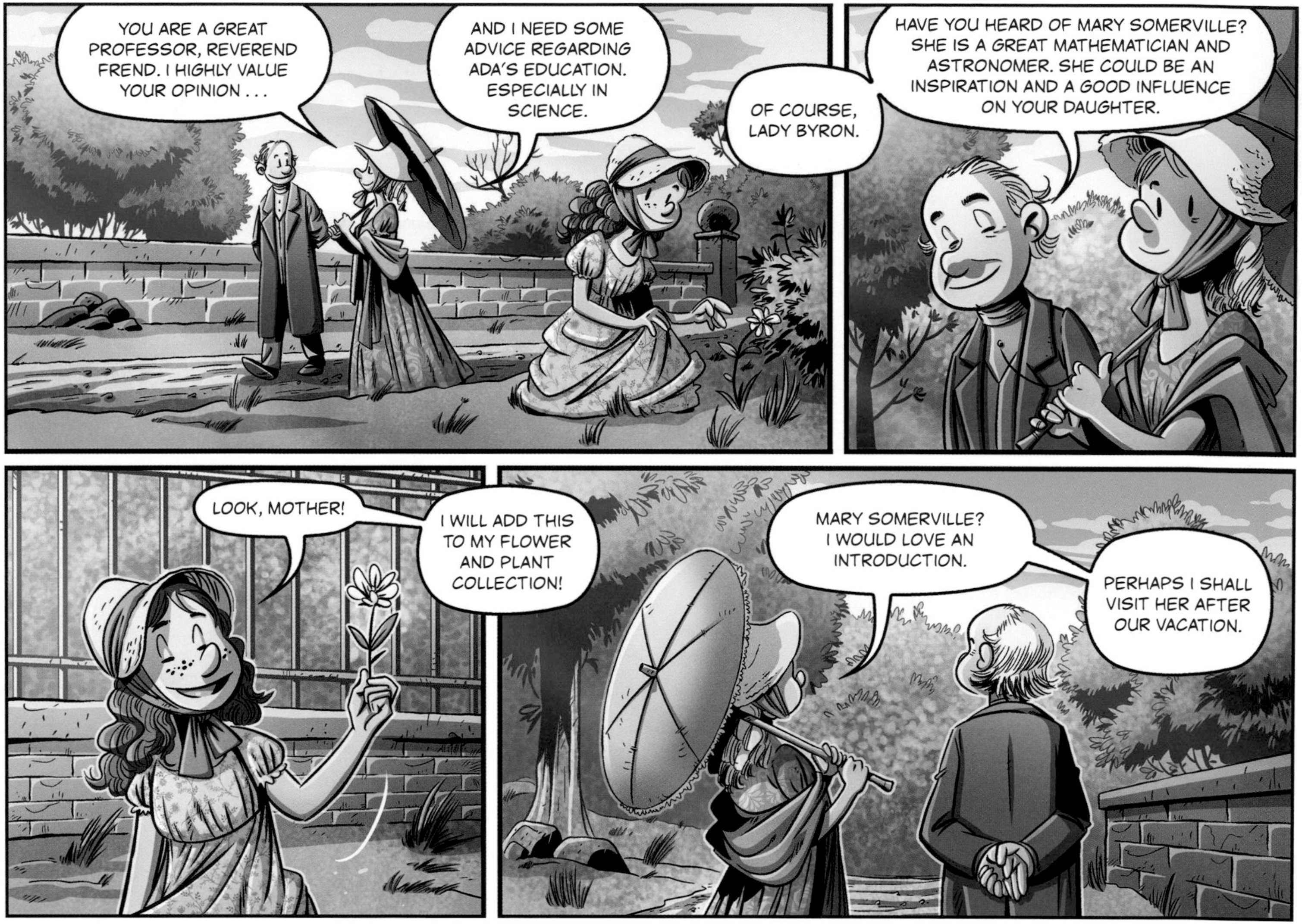

YOU ARE A GREAT PROFESSOR, REVEREND FREND. I HIGHLY VALUE YOUR OPINION . . .
AND I NEED SOME ADVICE REGARDING ADA'S EDUCATION. ESPECIALLY IN SCIENCE.
OF COURSE, LADY BYRON.
HAVE YOU HEARD OF MARY SOMERVILLE? SHE IS A GREAT MATHEMATICIAN AND ASTRONOMER. SHE COULD BE AN INSPIRATION AND A GOOD INFLUENCE ON YOUR DAUGHTER.
LOOK, MOTHER!
I WILL ADD THIS TO MY FLOWER AND PLANT COLLECTION!
MARY SOMERVILLE? I WOULD LOVE AN INTRODUCTION.
PERHAPS I SHALL VISIT HER AFTER OUR VACATION.

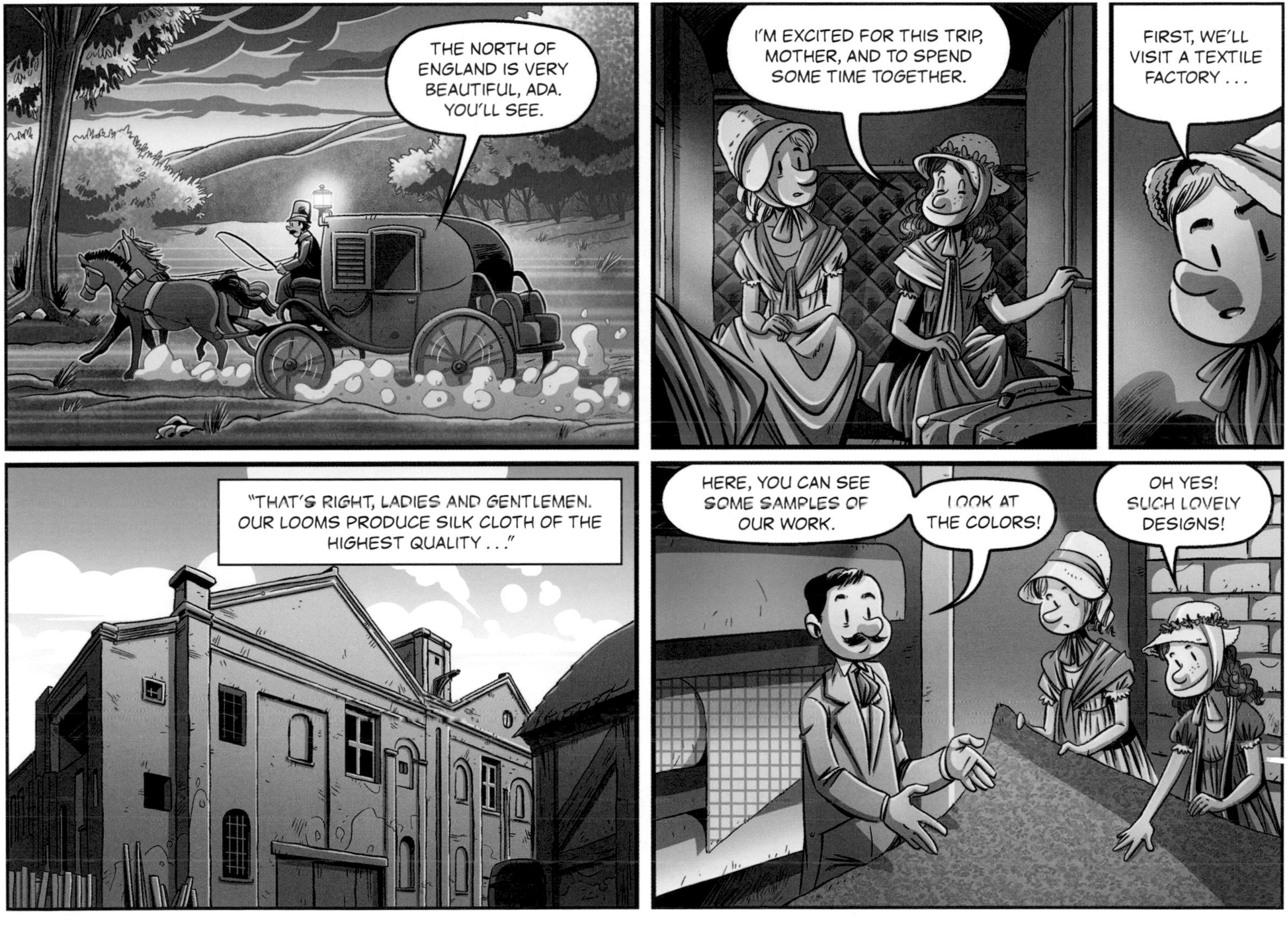
THE NORTH OF ENGLAND IS VERY BEAUTIFUL, ADA. YOU'LL SEE.
I'M EXCITED FOR THIS TRIP, MOTHER, AND TO SPEND SOME TIME TOGETHER.
FIRST, WE'LL VISIT A TEXTILE FACTORY . . .
"THAT'S RIGHT, LADIES AND GENTLEMEN. OUR LOOMS PRODUCE SILK CLOTH OF THE HIGHEST QUALITY . . ."
HERE, YOU CAN SEE SOME SAMPLES OF OUR WORK.
LOOK AT THE COLORS!
OH YES! SUCH LOVELY DESIGNS!

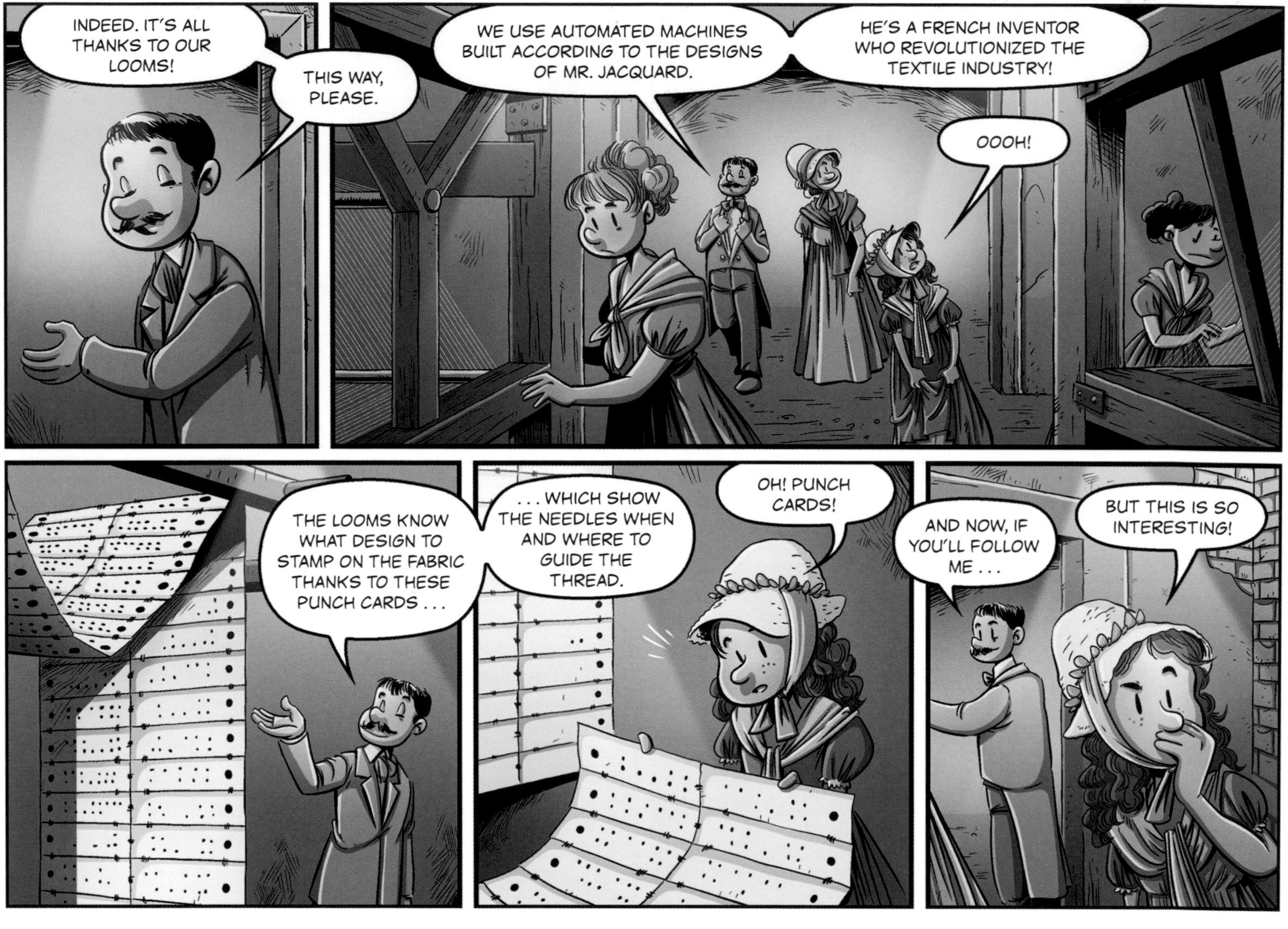
INDEED. IT'S ALL THANKS TO OUR LOOMS!
THIS WAY, PLEASE.
WE USE AUTOMATED MACHINES BUILT ACCORDING TO THE DESIGNS OF MR. JACQUARD.
HE'S A FRENCH INVENTOR WHO REVOLUTIONIZED THE TEXTILE INDUSTRY!
OOOH!
THE LOOMS KNOW WHAT DESIGN TO STAMP ON THE FABRIC THANKS TO THESE PUNCH CARDS . . .
. . . WHICH SHOW THE NEEDLES WHEN AND WHERE TO GUIDE THE THREAD.
OH! PUNCH CARDS!
AND NOW, IF YOU'LL FOLLOW ME . . .
BUT THIS IS SO INTERESTING!

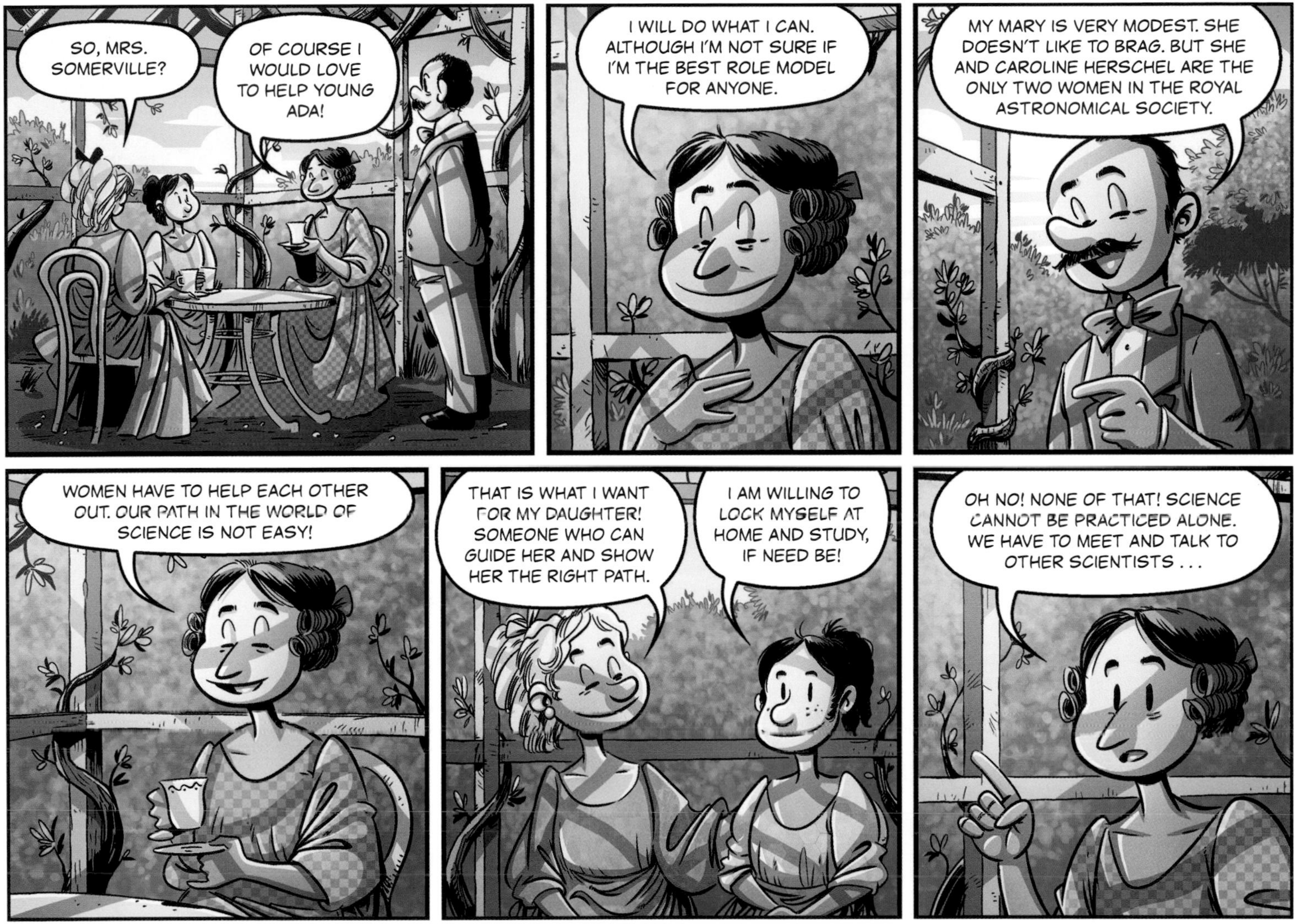
SO, MRS. SOMERVILLE?
OF COURSE I WOULD LOVE TO HELP YOUNG ADA!
I WILL DO WHAT I CAN. ALTHOUGH I'M NOT SURE IF I'M THE BEST ROLE MODEL FOR ANYONE.
MY MARY IS VERY MODEST. SHE DOESN'T LIKE TO BRAG. BUT SHE AND CAROLINE HERSCHEL ARE THE ONLY TWO WOMEN IN THE ROYAL ASTRONOMICAL SOCIETY.
WOMEN HAVE TO HELP EACH OTHER OUT. OUR PATH IN THE WORLD OF SCIENCE IS NOT EASY!
THAT IS WHAT I WANT FOR MY DAUGHTER! SOMEONE WHO CAN GUIDE HER AND SHOW HER THE RIGHT PATH.
I AM WILLING TO LOCK MYSELF AT HOME AND STUDY, IF NEED BE!
OH NO! NONE OF THAT! SCIENCE CANNOT BE PRACTICED ALONE. WE HAVE TO MEET AND TALK TO OTHER SCIENTISTS . . .

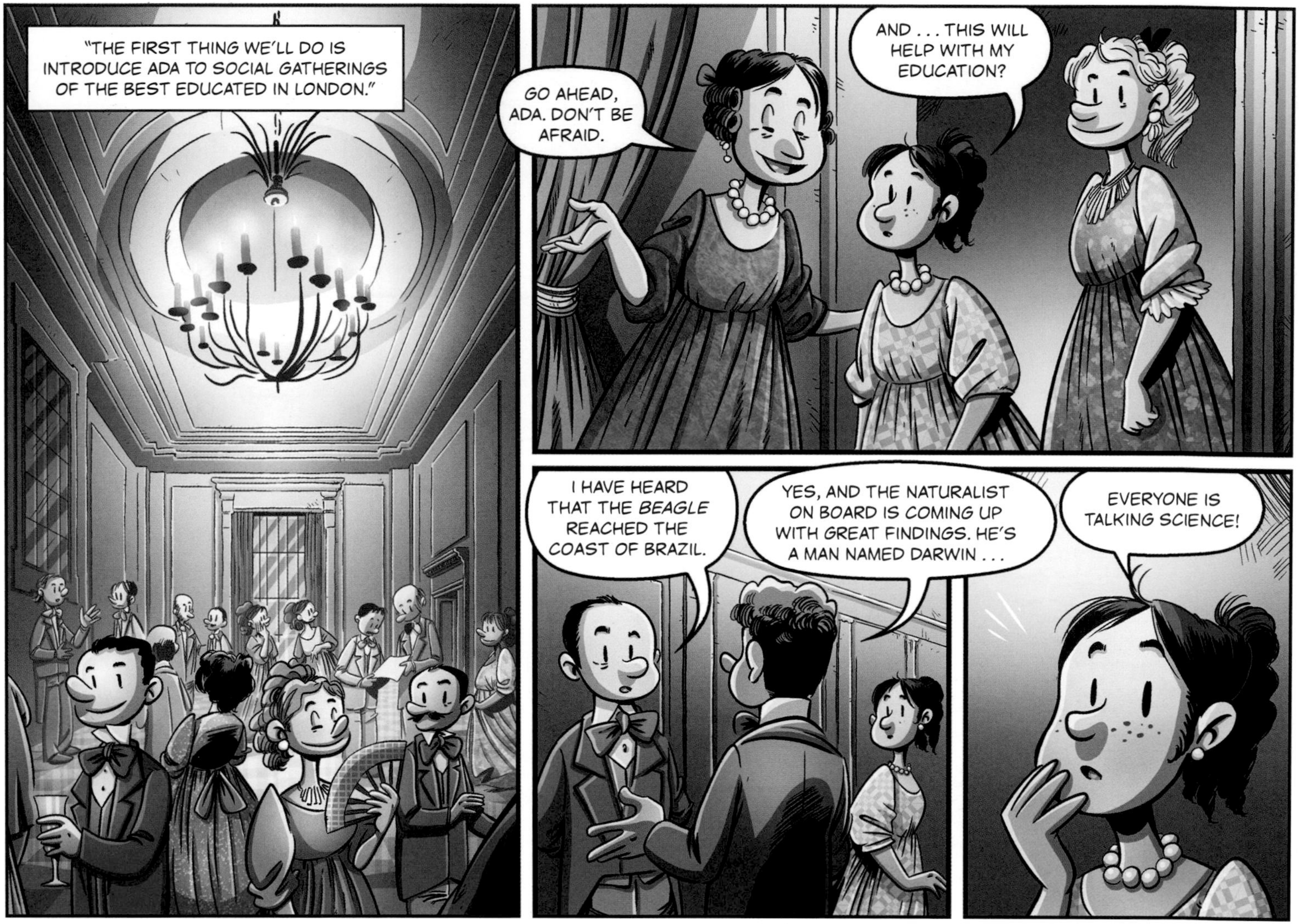
"THE FIRST THING WE'LL DO IS INTRODUCE ADA TO SOCIAL GATHERINGS OF THE BEST EDUCATED IN LONDON."
GO AHEAD, ADA. DON'T BE AFRAID.
AND . . . THIS WILL HELP WITH MY EDUCATION?
I HAVE HEARD THAT THE *BEAGLE* REACHED THE COAST OF BRAZIL.
YES, AND THE NATURALIST ON BOARD IS COMING UP WITH GREAT FINDINGS. HE'S A MAN NAMED DARWIN . . .
EVERYONE IS TALKING SCIENCE!

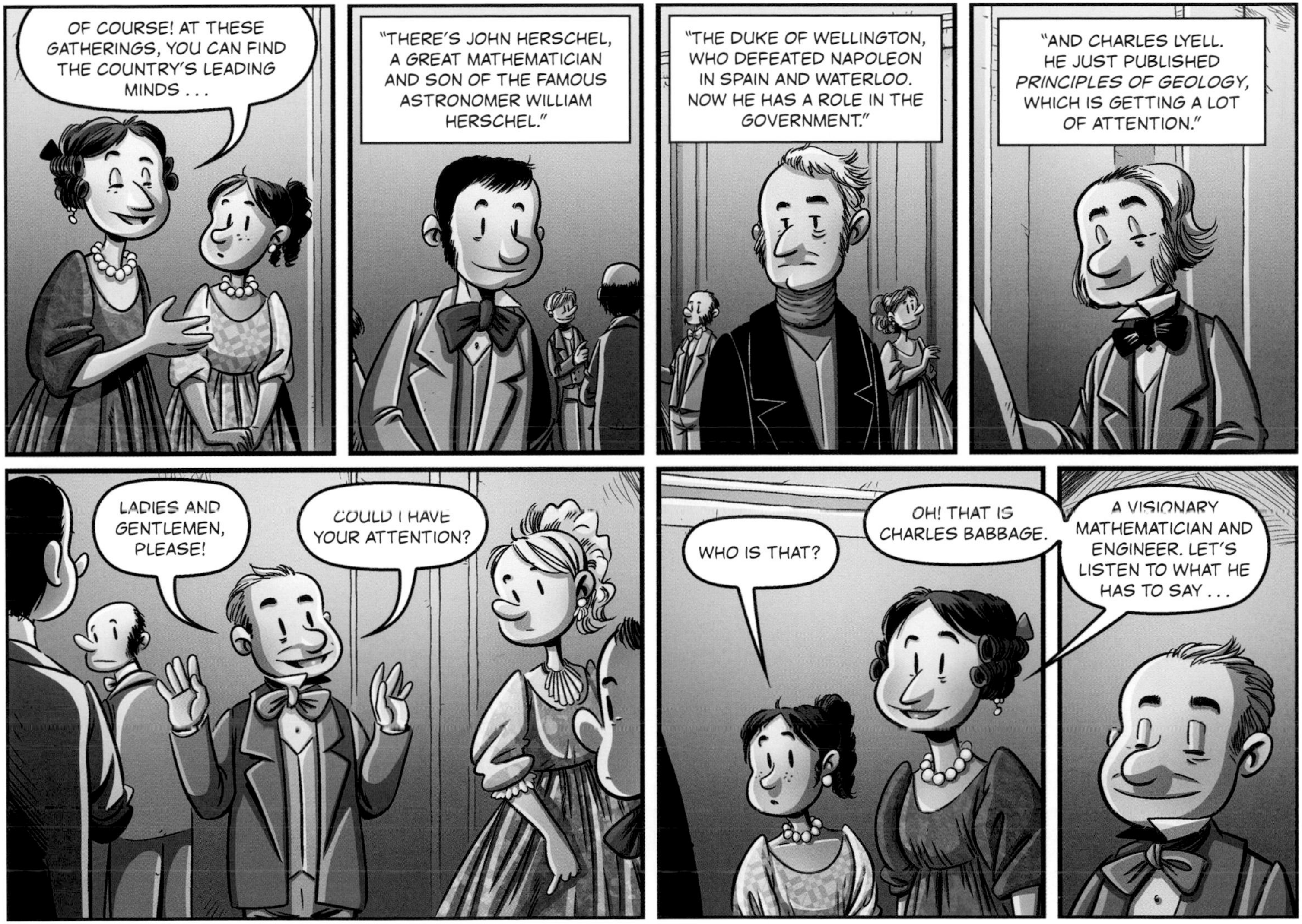
OF COURSE! AT THESE GATHERINGS, YOU CAN FIND THE COUNTRY'S LEADING MINDS . . .
"THERE'S JOHN HERSCHEL, A GREAT MATHEMATICIAN AND SON OF THE FAMOUS ASTRONOMER WILLIAM HERSCHEL."
"THE DUKE OF WELLINGTON, WHO DEFEATED NAPOLEON IN SPAIN AND WATERLOO. NOW HE HAS A ROLE IN THE GOVERNMENT."
"AND CHARLES LYELL. HE JUST PUBLISHED *PRINCIPLES OF GEOLOGY*, WHICH IS GETTING A LOT OF ATTENTION."
LADIES AND GENTLEMEN, PLEASE!
COULD I HAVE YOUR ATTENTION?
WHO IS THAT?
OH! THAT IS CHARLES BABBAGE.
A VISIONARY MATHEMATICIAN AND ENGINEER. LET'S LISTEN TO WHAT HE HAS TO SAY . . .

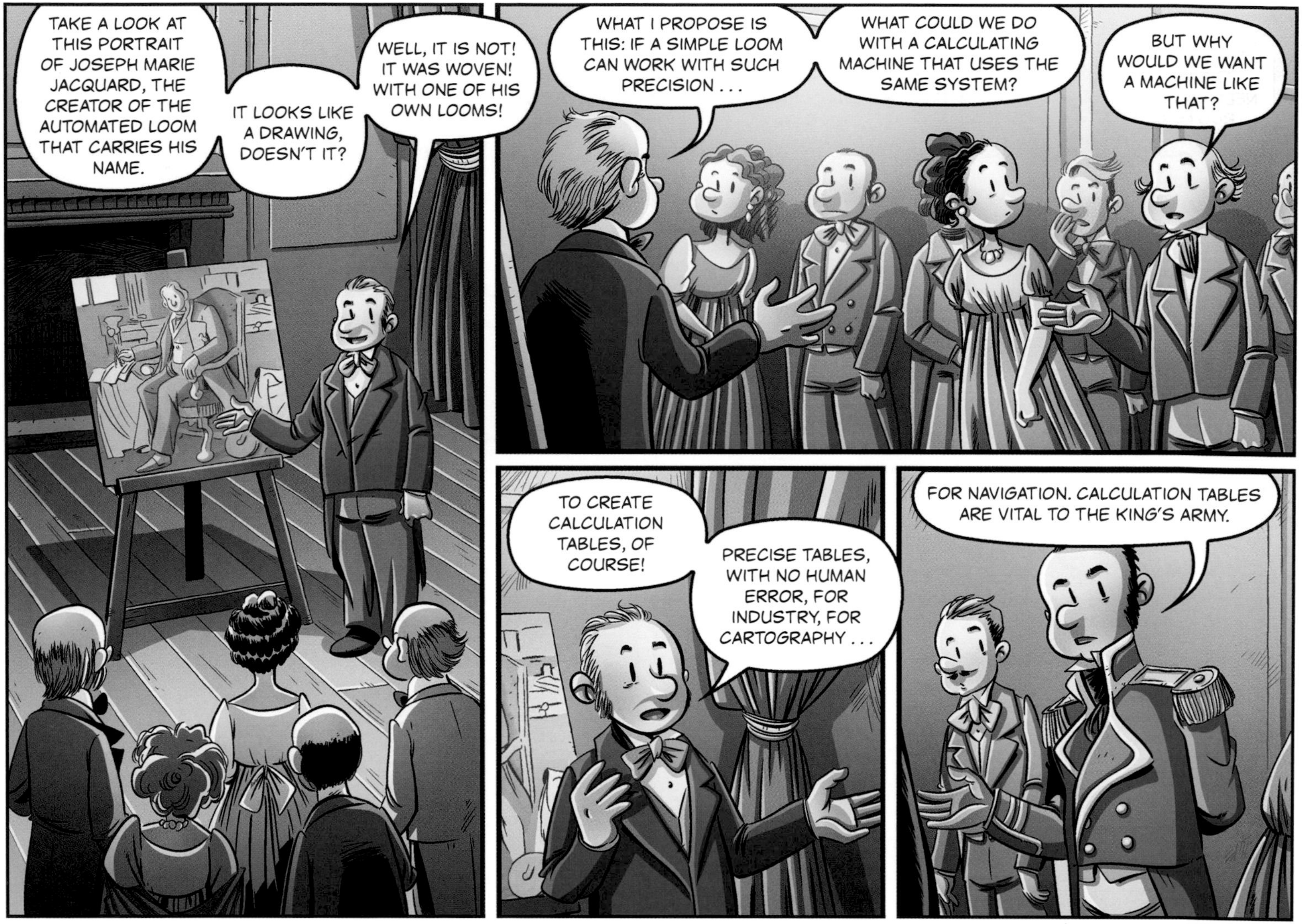
TAKE A LOOK AT THIS PORTRAIT OF JOSEPH MARIE JACQUARD, THE CREATOR OF THE AUTOMATED LOOM THAT CARRIES HIS NAME.
IT LOOKS LIKE A DRAWING, DOESN'T IT?
WELL, IT IS NOT! IT WAS WOVEN! WITH ONE OF HIS OWN LOOMS!
WHAT I PROPOSE IS THIS: IF A SIMPLE LOOM CAN WORK WITH SUCH PRECISION . . .
WHAT COULD WE DO WITH A CALCULATING MACHINE THAT USES THE SAME SYSTEM?
BUT WHY WOULD WE WANT A MACHINE LIKE THAT?
TO CREATE CALCULATION TABLES, OF COURSE!
PRECISE TABLES, WITH NO HUMAN ERROR, FOR INDUSTRY, FOR CARTOGRAPHY . . .
FOR NAVIGATION. CALCULATION TABLES ARE VITAL TO THE KING'S ARMY.

"WHEN OUR ARMY'S SHIPS SAIL THE WORLD'S OCEANS, THEY NEED MATHEMATICS TO SET THEIR ROUTE AND ARRIVE AT PORT."

"SAILORS MEASURE THE POSITION OF THE STARS USING THEIR SEXTANTS . . ."

". . . AND THEN PERFORM THE PROCESS THAT WILL LET THEM KNOW THEIR COURSE."

"BUT THESE ARE COMPLICATED CALCULATIONS. IT WOULD TAKE THEM FOREVER TO FIND THE ANSWER ANEW EACH TIME."

"INSTEAD, THEY CONSULT PREVIOUSLY MADE CHARTS."

LET'S SEE.

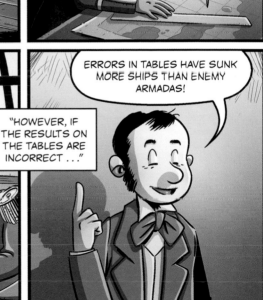

"HOWEVER, IF THE RESULTS ON THE TABLES ARE INCORRECT . . ."

ERRORS IN TABLES HAVE SUNK MORE SHIPS THAN ENEMY ARMADAS!

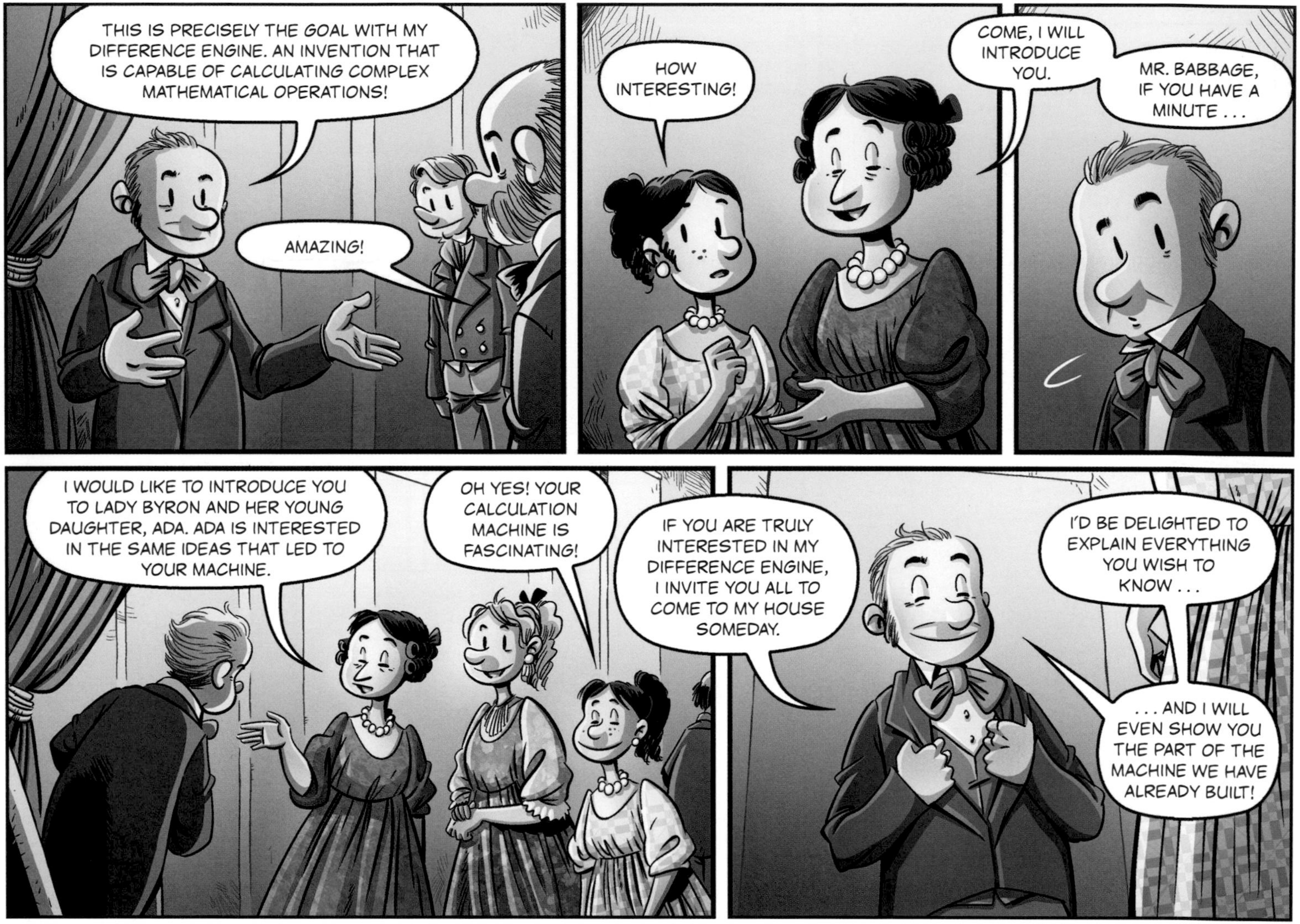
THIS IS PRECISELY THE GOAL WITH MY DIFFERENCE ENGINE. AN INVENTION THAT IS CAPABLE OF CALCULATING COMPLEX MATHEMATICAL OPERATIONS!
AMAZING!
HOW INTERESTING!
COME, I WILL INTRODUCE YOU.
MR. BABBAGE, IF YOU HAVE A MINUTE . . .
I WOULD LIKE TO INTRODUCE YOU TO LADY BYRON AND HER YOUNG DAUGHTER, ADA. ADA IS INTERESTED IN THE SAME IDEAS THAT LED TO YOUR MACHINE.
OH YES! YOUR CALCULATION MACHINE IS FASCINATING!
IF YOU ARE TRULY INTERESTED IN MY DIFFERENCE ENGINE, I INVITE YOU ALL TO COME TO MY HOUSE SOMEDAY.
I'D BE DELIGHTED TO EXPLAIN EVERYTHING YOU WISH TO KNOW . . .
. . . AND I WILL EVEN SHOW YOU THE PART OF THE MACHINE WE HAVE ALREADY BUILT!

CHARLES BABBAGE'S HOUSE

WELCOME! COME ON IN.

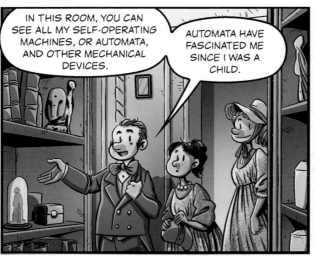

IN THIS ROOM, YOU CAN SEE ALL MY SELF-OPERATING MACHINES, OR AUTOMATA, AND OTHER MECHANICAL DEVICES.

AUTOMATA HAVE FASCINATED ME SINCE I WAS A CHILD.

I BOUGHT THESE TWO AT A CIRCUS NEAR MY PARENTS' HOUSE. THEY ARE EXQUISITE!

I HAVE ALWAYS BEEN INTERESTED IN MATHEMATICS AND ENGINEERING. DID YOU KNOW THAT I TAUGHT AT CAMBRIDGE? I HELD THE SAME CHAIR AS SIR ISAAC NEWTON!

"IT WAS IN CAMBRIDGE WHERE, ALONG WITH MY FRIENDS JOHN HERSCHEL AND GEORGE PEACOCK, I FOUNDED THE ANALYTICAL SOCIETY TO REFORM MATHEMATICS . . ."

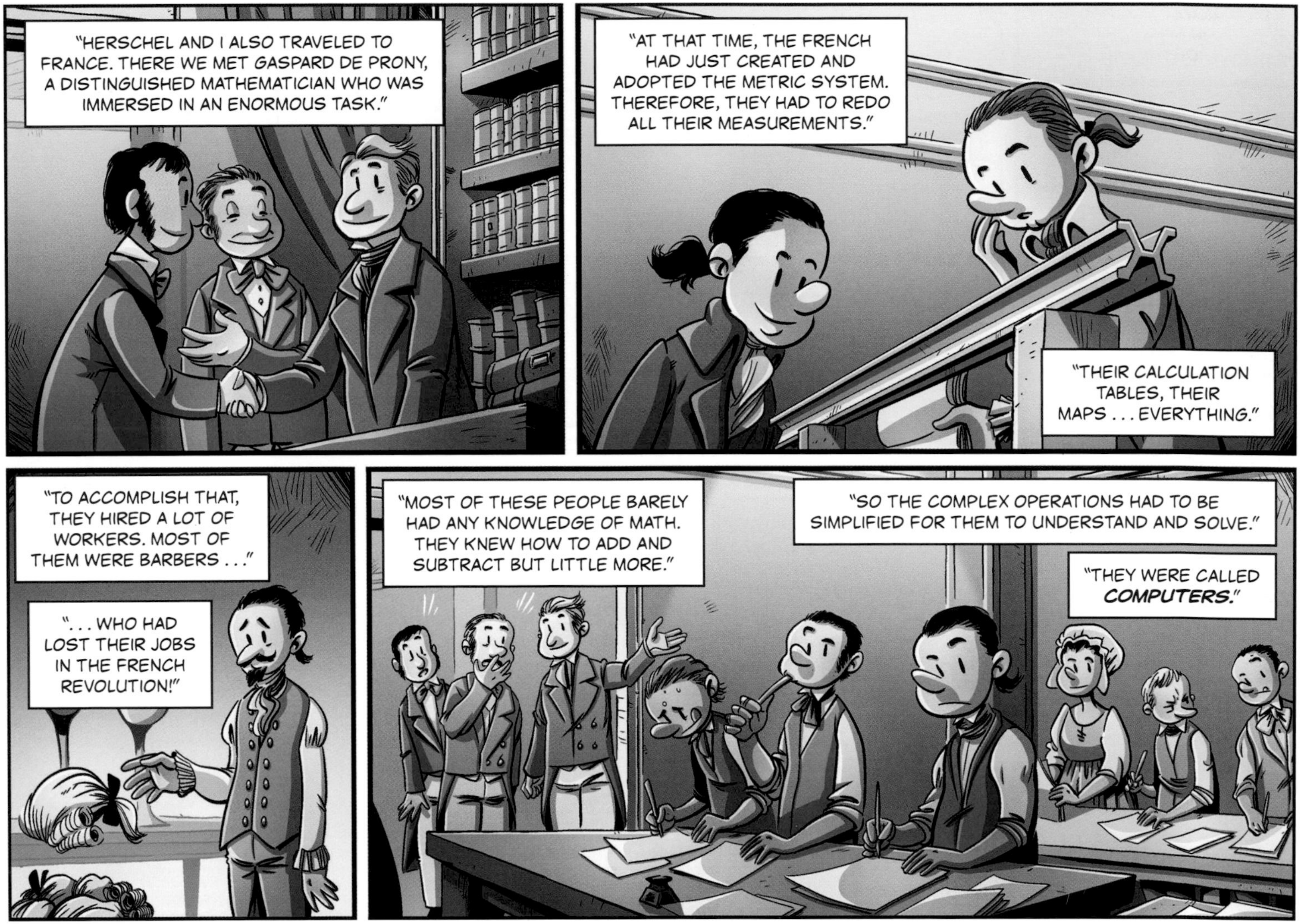
"HERSCHEL AND I ALSO TRAVELED TO FRANCE. THERE WE MET GASPARD DE PRONY, A DISTINGUISHED MATHEMATICIAN WHO WAS IMMERSED IN AN ENORMOUS TASK."
"AT THAT TIME, THE FRENCH HAD JUST CREATED AND ADOPTED THE METRIC SYSTEM. THEREFORE, THEY HAD TO REDO ALL THEIR MEASUREMENTS."
"THEIR CALCULATION TABLES, THEIR MAPS . . . EVERYTHING."
"TO ACCOMPLISH THAT, THEY HIRED A LOT OF WORKERS. MOST OF THEM WERE BARBERS . . ."
". . . WHO HAD LOST THEIR JOBS IN THE FRENCH REVOLUTION!"
"MOST OF THESE PEOPLE BARELY HAD ANY KNOWLEDGE OF MATH. THEY KNEW HOW TO ADD AND SUBTRACT BUT LITTLE MORE."
"SO THE COMPLEX OPERATIONS HAD TO BE SIMPLIFIED FOR THEM TO UNDERSTAND AND SOLVE."
"THEY WERE CALLED ***COMPUTERS.***"

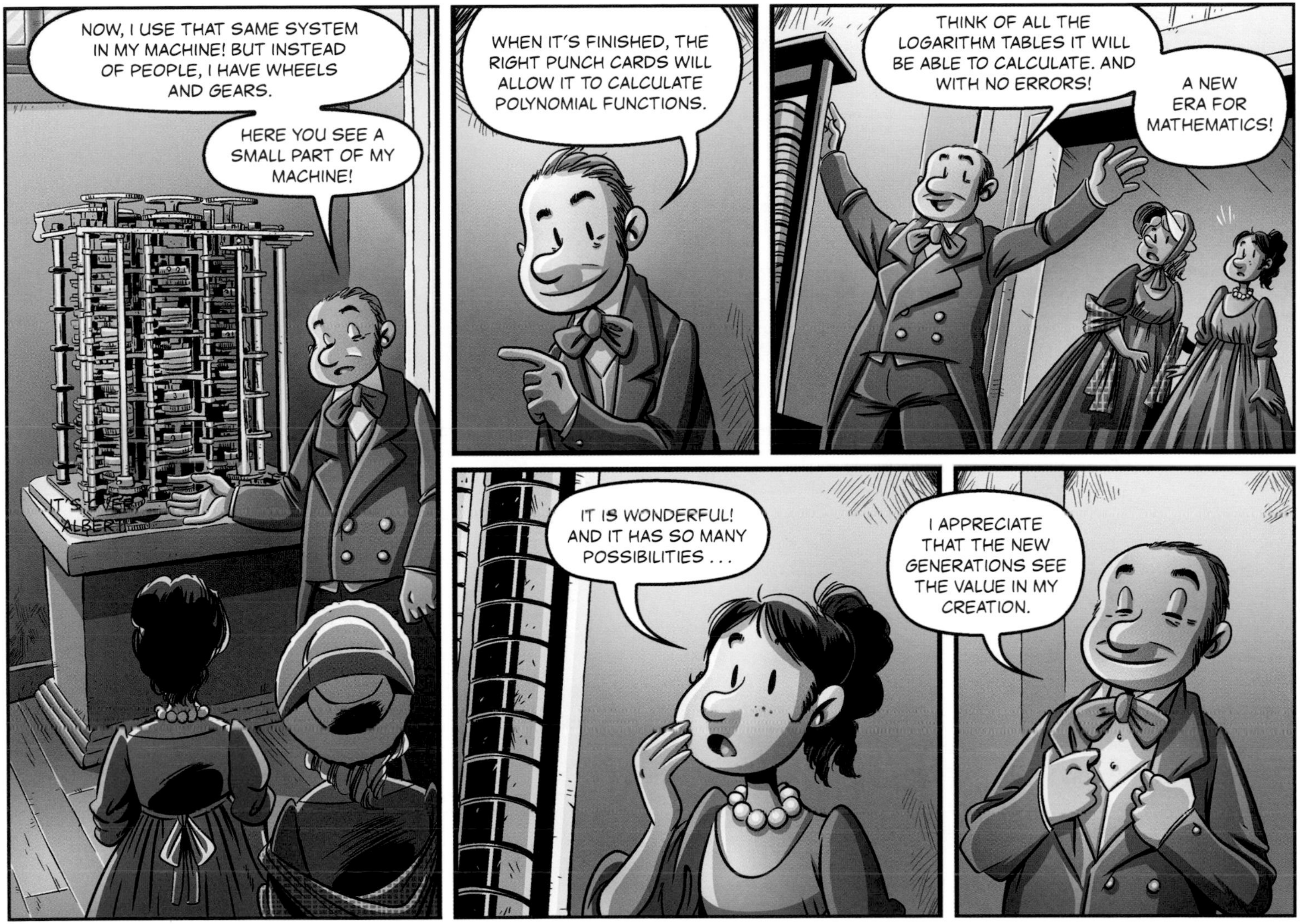
NOW, I USE THAT SAME SYSTEM IN MY MACHINE! BUT INSTEAD OF PEOPLE, I HAVE WHEELS AND GEARS.
HERE YOU SEE A SMALL PART OF MY MACHINE!
WHEN IT'S FINISHED, THE RIGHT PUNCH CARDS WILL ALLOW IT TO CALCULATE POLYNOMIAL FUNCTIONS.
THINK OF ALL THE LOGARITHM TABLES IT WILL BE ABLE TO CALCULATE. AND WITH NO ERRORS!
A NEW ERA FOR MATHEMATICS!
IT IS WONDERFUL! AND IT HAS SO MANY POSSIBILITIES . . .
I APPRECIATE THAT THE NEW GENERATIONS SEE THE VALUE IN MY CREATION.

I VALUE IT GREATLY! YOUR INVENTION IS INCREDIBLE.

I WANT TO KNOW ABOUT YOUR PROGRESS. WOULD YOU LET ME WRITE TO YOU AND ASK YOU QUESTIONS?

UH . . . YES, OF COURSE.

IF YOU WANT TO KNOW MORE ABOUT MY MACHINE, YOU COULD ALSO ATTEND LECTURES BY PROFESSOR DIONYSIUS LARDNER, A RENOWNED SPEAKER ON SCIENCE . . .

"I AM SURE YOU WILL FIND THEM COMPELLING."

Dionysius
Lardner
. . .
Difference
Engine

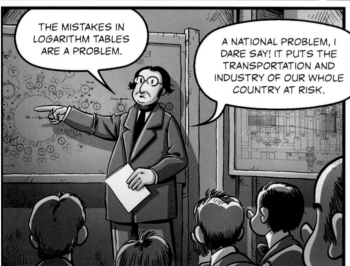

THE MISTAKES IN LOGARITHM TABLES ARE A PROBLEM.

A NATIONAL PROBLEM, I DARE SAY! IT PUTS THE TRANSPORTATION AND INDUSTRY OF OUR WHOLE COUNTRY AT RISK.

THE SOLUTION: CALCULATE THE TABLES USING THE DIFFERENCE ENGINE OF CHARLES BABBAGE.

HMM!

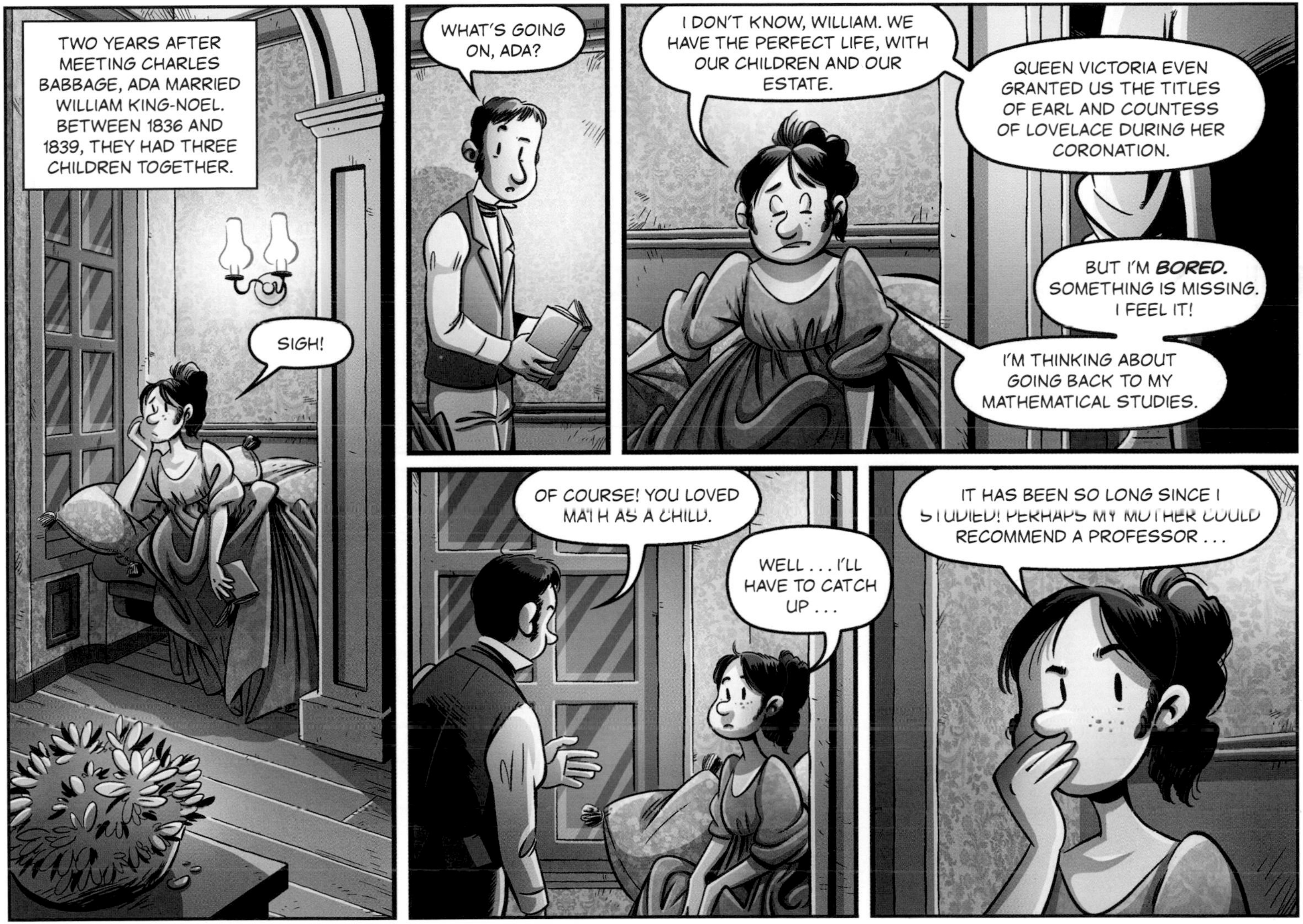
TWO YEARS AFTER MEETING CHARLES BABBAGE, ADA MARRIED WILLIAM KING-NOEL. BETWEEN 1836 AND 1839, THEY HAD THREE CHILDREN TOGETHER.
SIGH!
WHAT'S GOING ON, ADA?
I DON'T KNOW, WILLIAM. WE HAVE THE PERFECT LIFE, WITH OUR CHILDREN AND OUR ESTATE.
QUEEN VICTORIA EVEN GRANTED US THE TITLES OF EARL AND COUNTESS OF LOVELACE DURING HER CORONATION.
BUT I'M ***BORED.*** SOMETHING IS MISSING. I FEEL IT!
I'M THINKING ABOUT GOING BACK TO MY MATHEMATICAL STUDIES.
OF COURSE! YOU LOVED MATH AS A CHILD.
WELL . . . I'LL HAVE TO CATCH UP . . .
IT HAS BEEN SO LONG SINCE I STUDIED! PERHAPS MY MOTHER COULD RECOMMEND A PROFESSOR . . .

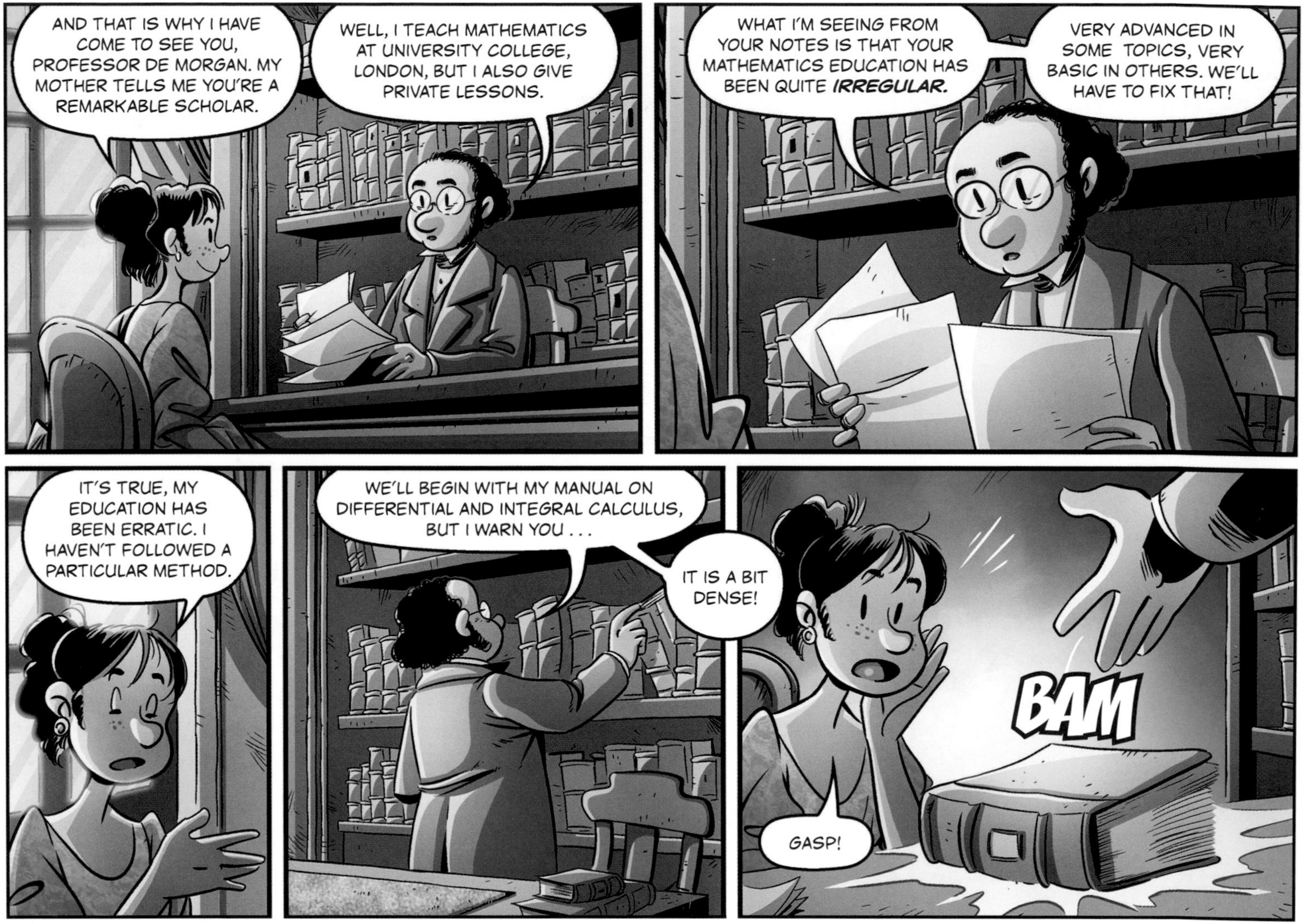
AND THAT IS WHY I HAVE COME TO SEE YOU, PROFESSOR DE MORGAN. MY MOTHER TELLS ME YOU'RE A REMARKABLE SCHOLAR.
WELL, I TEACH MATHEMATICS AT UNIVERSITY COLLEGE, LONDON, BUT I ALSO GIVE PRIVATE LESSONS.
WHAT I'M SEEING FROM YOUR NOTES IS THAT YOUR MATHEMATICS EDUCATION HAS BEEN QUITE ***IRREGULAR.***
VERY ADVANCED IN SOME TOPICS, VERY BASIC IN OTHERS. WE'LL HAVE TO FIX THAT!
IT'S TRUE, MY EDUCATION HAS BEEN ERRATIC. I HAVEN'T FOLLOWED A PARTICULAR METHOD.
WE'LL BEGIN WITH MY MANUAL ON DIFFERENTIAL AND INTEGRAL CALCULUS, BUT I WARN YOU . . .
IT IS A BIT DENSE!
BAM
GASP!

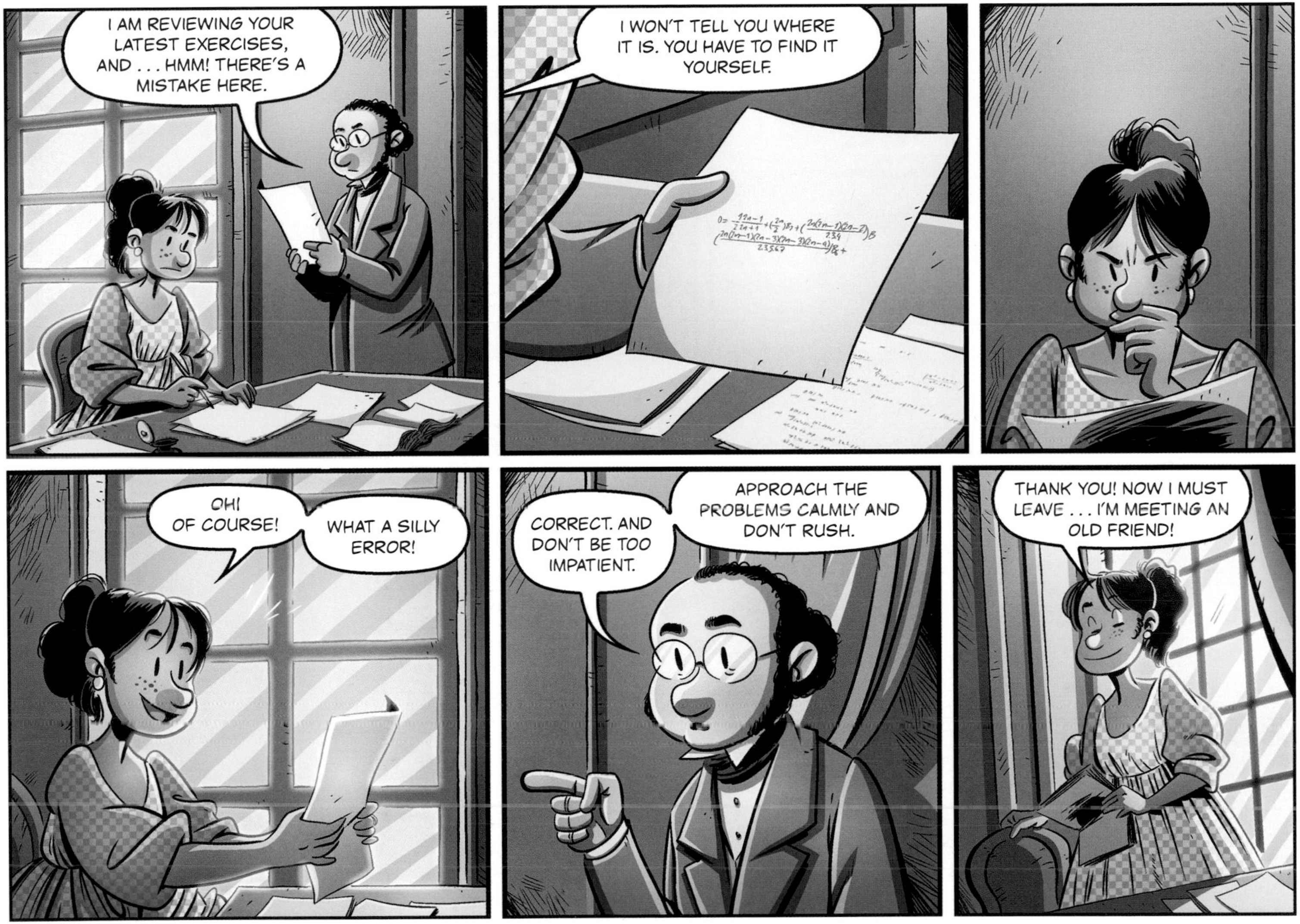
I AM REVIEWING YOUR LATEST EXERCISES, AND . . . HMM! THERE'S A MISTAKE HERE.
I WON'T TELL YOU WHERE IT IS. YOU HAVE TO FIND IT YOURSELF.
OH! OF COURSE!
WHAT A SILLY ERROR!
CORRECT. AND DON'T BE TOO IMPATIENT.
APPROACH THE PROBLEMS CALMLY AND DON'T RUSH.
THANK YOU! NOW I MUST LEAVE . . . I'M MEETING AN OLD FRIEND!

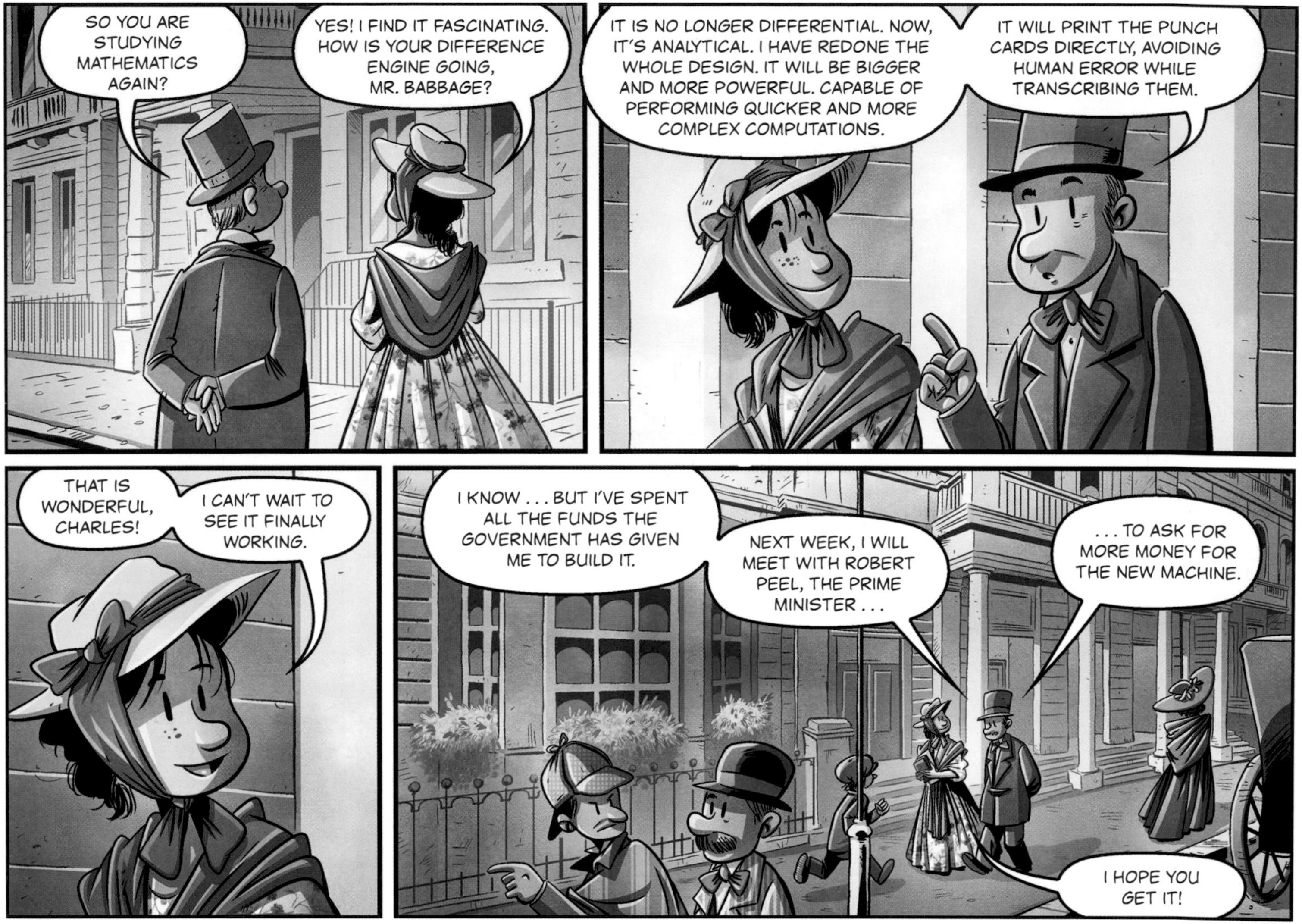
SO YOU ARE STUDYING MATHEMATICS AGAIN?
YES! I FIND IT FASCINATING. HOW IS YOUR DIFFERENCE ENGINE GOING, MR. BABBAGE?
IT IS NO LONGER DIFFERENTIAL. NOW, IT'S ANALYTICAL. I HAVE REDONE THE WHOLE DESIGN. IT WILL BE BIGGER AND MORE POWERFUL. CAPABLE OF PERFORMING QUICKER AND MORE COMPLEX COMPUTATIONS.
IT WILL PRINT THE PUNCH CARDS DIRECTLY, AVOIDING HUMAN ERROR WHILE TRANSCRIBING THEM.
THAT IS WONDERFUL, CHARLES!
I CAN'T WAIT TO SEE IT FINALLY WORKING.
I KNOW . . . BUT I'VE SPENT ALL THE FUNDS THE GOVERNMENT HAS GIVEN ME TO BUILD IT.
NEXT WEEK, I WILL MEET WITH ROBERT PEEL, THE PRIME MINISTER . . .
. . . TO ASK FOR MORE MONEY FOR THE NEW MACHINE.
I HOPE YOU GET IT!

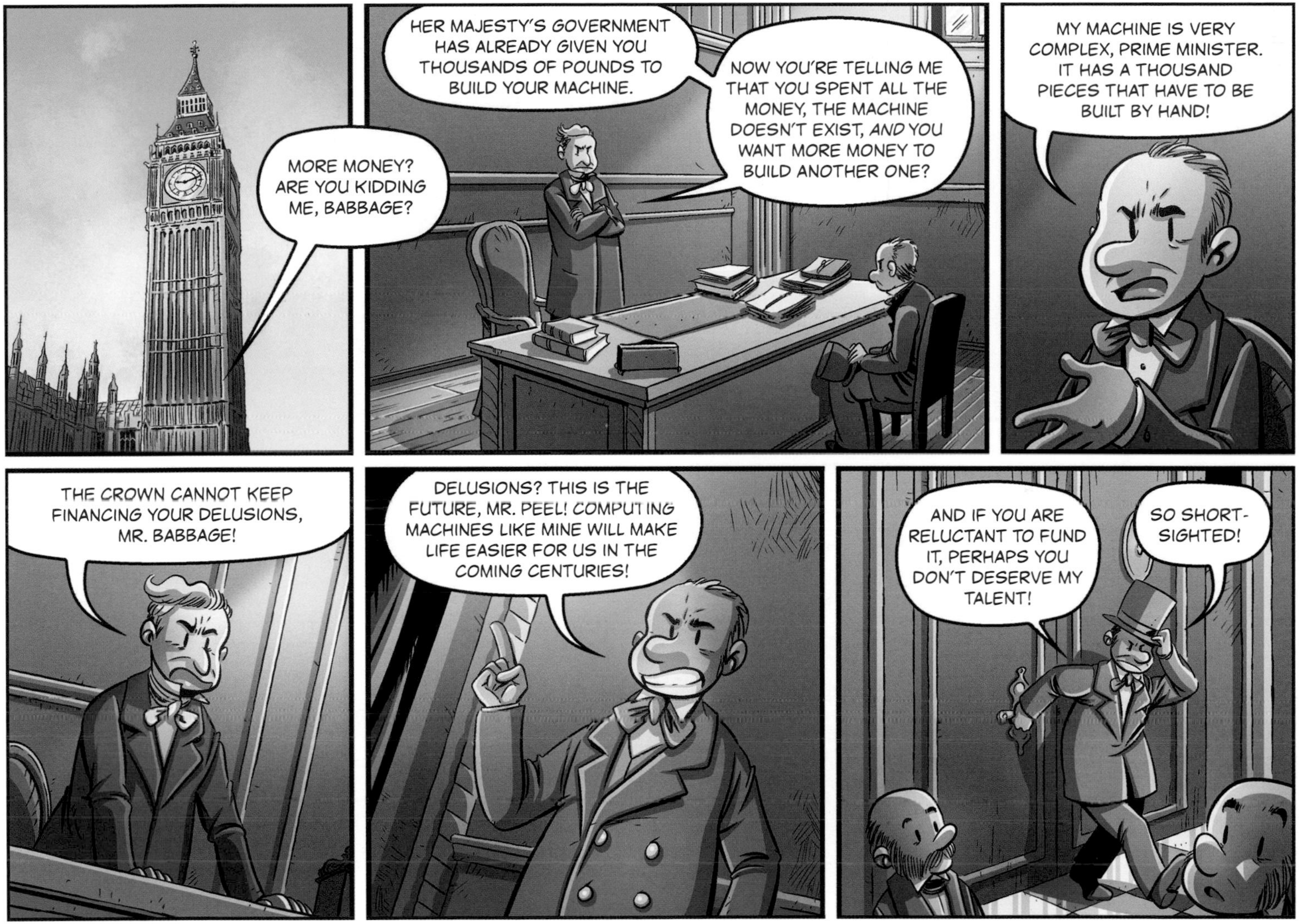
MORE MONEY? ARE YOU KIDDING ME, BABBAGE?
HER MAJESTY'S GOVERNMENT HAS ALREADY GIVEN YOU THOUSANDS OF POUNDS TO BUILD YOUR MACHINE.
NOW YOU'RE TELLING ME THAT YOU SPENT ALL THE MONEY, THE MACHINE DOESN'T EXIST, *AND* YOU WANT MORE MONEY TO BUILD ANOTHER ONE?
MY MACHINE IS VERY COMPLEX, PRIME MINISTER. IT HAS A THOUSAND PIECES THAT HAVE TO BE BUILT BY HAND!
THE CROWN CANNOT KEEP FINANCING YOUR DELUSIONS, MR. BABBAGE!
DELUSIONS? THIS IS THE FUTURE, MR. PEEL! COMPUTING MACHINES LIKE MINE WILL MAKE LIFE EASIER FOR US IN THE COMING CENTURIES!
AND IF YOU ARE RELUCTANT TO FUND IT, PERHAPS YOU DON'T DESERVE MY TALENT!
SO SHORT-SIGHTED!

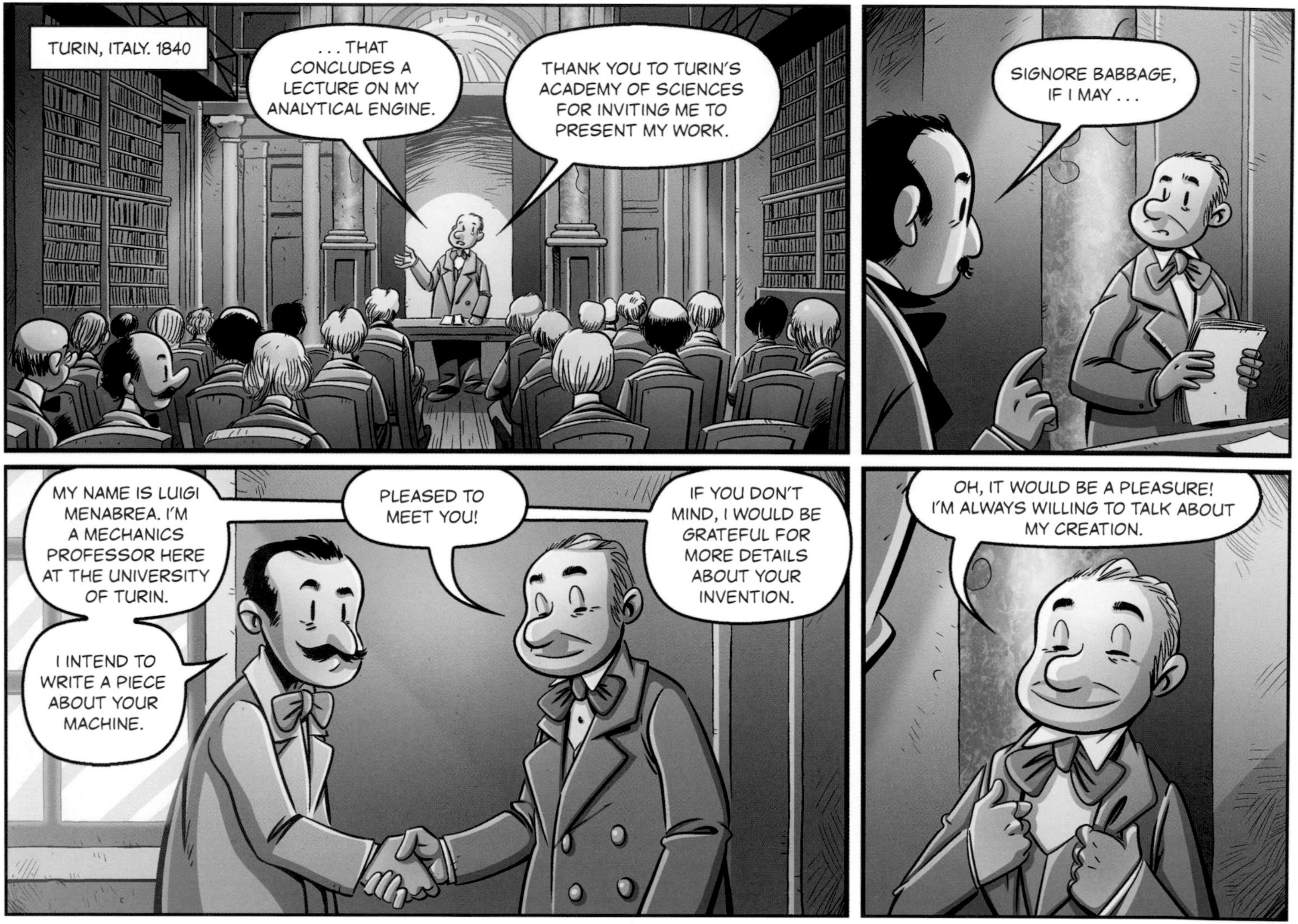

TURIN, ITALY. 1840
. . . THAT CONCLUDES A LECTURE ON MY ANALYTICAL ENGINE.
THANK YOU TO TURIN'S ACADEMY OF SCIENCES FOR INVITING ME TO PRESENT MY WORK.
SIGNORE BABBAGE, IF I MAY . . .
MY NAME IS LUIGI MENABREA. I'M A MECHANICS PROFESSOR HERE AT THE UNIVERSITY OF TURIN.
I INTEND TO WRITE A PIECE ABOUT YOUR MACHINE.
PLEASED TO MEET YOU!
IF YOU DON'T MIND, I WOULD BE GRATEFUL FOR MORE DETAILS ABOUT YOUR INVENTION.
OH, IT WOULD BE A PLEASURE! I'M ALWAYS WILLING TO TALK ABOUT MY CREATION.

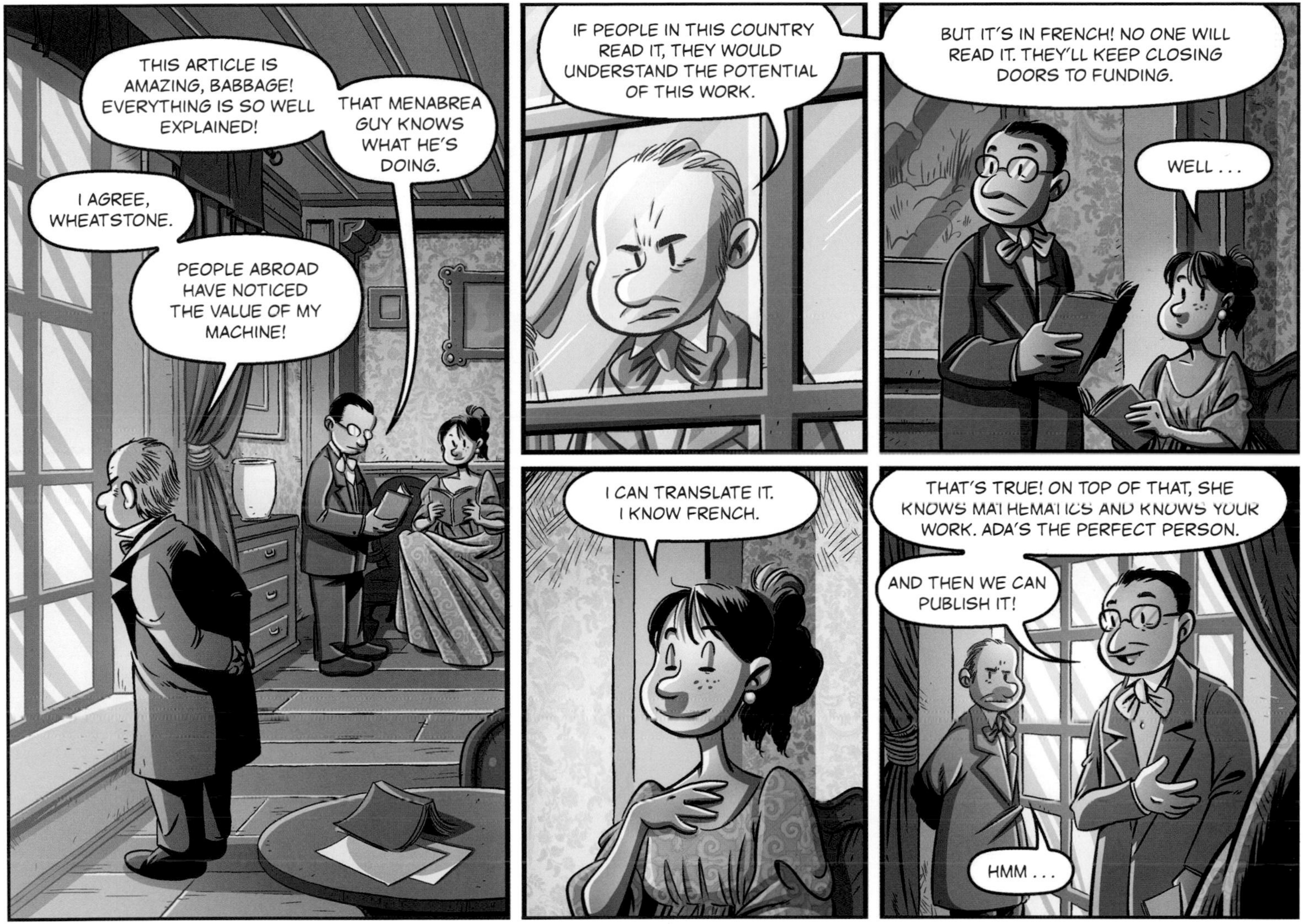
THIS ARTICLE IS AMAZING, BABBAGE! EVERYTHING IS SO WELL EXPLAINED!
THAT MENABREA GUY KNOWS WHAT HE'S DOING.
I AGREE, WHEATSTONE.
PEOPLE ABROAD HAVE NOTICED THE VALUE OF MY MACHINE!
IF PEOPLE IN THIS COUNTRY READ IT, THEY WOULD UNDERSTAND THE POTENTIAL OF THIS WORK.
BUT IT'S IN FRENCH! NO ONE WILL READ IT. THEY'LL KEEP CLOSING DOORS TO FUNDING.
WELL . . .
I CAN TRANSLATE IT. I KNOW FRENCH.
THAT'S TRUE! ON TOP OF THAT, SHE KNOWS MATHEMATICS AND KNOWS YOUR WORK. ADA'S THE PERFECT PERSON.
AND THEN WE CAN PUBLISH IT!
HMM . . .

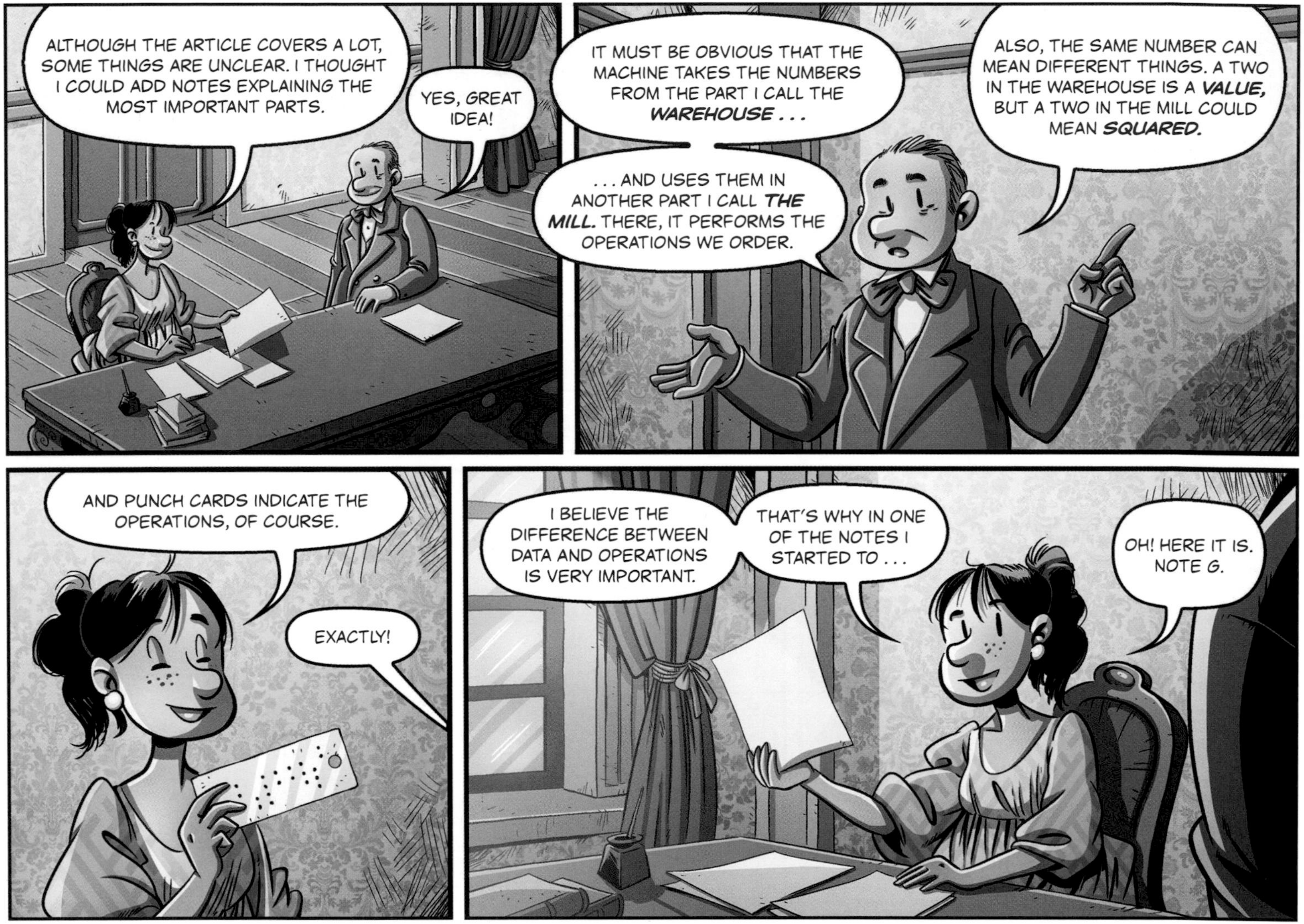
ALTHOUGH THE ARTICLE COVERS A LOT, SOME THINGS ARE UNCLEAR. I THOUGHT I COULD ADD NOTES EXPLAINING THE MOST IMPORTANT PARTS.
YES, GREAT IDEA!
IT MUST BE OBVIOUS THAT THE MACHINE TAKES THE NUMBERS FROM THE PART I CALL THE ***WAREHOUSE . . .***
. . . AND USES THEM IN ANOTHER PART I CALL ***THE MILL.*** THERE, IT PERFORMS THE OPERATIONS WE ORDER.
ALSO, THE SAME NUMBER CAN MEAN DIFFERENT THINGS. A TWO IN THE WAREHOUSE IS A ***VALUE,*** BUT A TWO IN THE MILL COULD MEAN ***SQUARED.***
AND PUNCH CARDS INDICATE THE OPERATIONS, OF COURSE.
EXACTLY!
I BELIEVE THE DIFFERENCE BETWEEN DATA AND OPERATIONS IS VERY IMPORTANT.
THAT'S WHY IN ONE OF THE NOTES I STARTED TO . . .
OH! HERE IT IS. NOTE G.

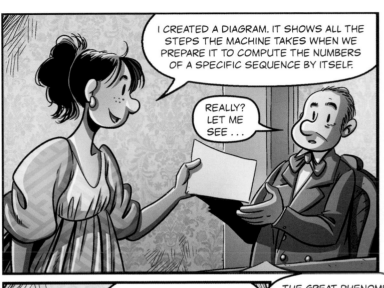

I CREATED A DIAGRAM. IT SHOWS ALL THE STEPS THE MACHINE TAKES WHEN WE PREPARE IT TO COMPUTE THE NUMBERS OF A SPECIFIC SEQUENCE BY ITSELF.

REALLY? LET ME SEE . . .

IT'S AN EXAMPLE OF HOW THE MACHINE CAN WORK ON ITS OWN AFTER THE CORRECT MATHEMATICAL INSTRUCTIONS.

AMAZING!

AND THIS IS JUST THE BEGINNING!

THE ANALYTICAL MACHINE WEAVES ALGEBRAICAL PATTERNS JUST LIKE JACQUARD'S LOOMS WEAVE LEAVES AND FLOWERS.

THE GREAT PHENOMENA OF THE NATURAL WORLD ARE EXPRESSED THROUGH MATHEMATICS.

THINK ABOUT IT, CHARLES . . .

THE MACHINE WON'T ONLY BUILD TABLES . . . IT COULD EVEN WRITE MUSIC!

OH! REALLY?

ADA? ARE YOU STILL WORKING ON THE TRANSLATION? I THOUGHT YOU HAD FINISHED IT.

OH, YES, IT'S FINISHED.

I WAS WONDERING IF IT'S APPROPRIATE FOR A LADY IN MY POSITION TO SIGN HER NAME ON SUCH AN ARTICLE . . .

AND I DON'T KNOW.

WHY WOULDN'T IT BE? DIDN'T YOU TRANSLATE IT? YOU EVEN ADDED NOTES. YOU MADE IT BETTER!

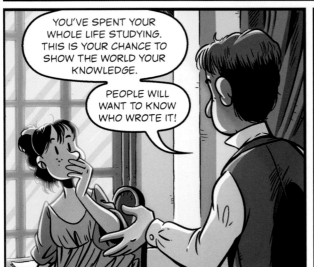

YOU'VE SPENT YOUR WHOLE LIFE STUDYING. THIS IS YOUR CHANCE TO SHOW THE WORLD YOUR KNOWLEDGE.

PEOPLE WILL WANT TO KNOW WHO WROTE IT!

IF YOU DON'T WANT TO SIGN YOUR FULL NAME, AT LEAST WRITE YOUR INITIALS.

ALL RIGHT!

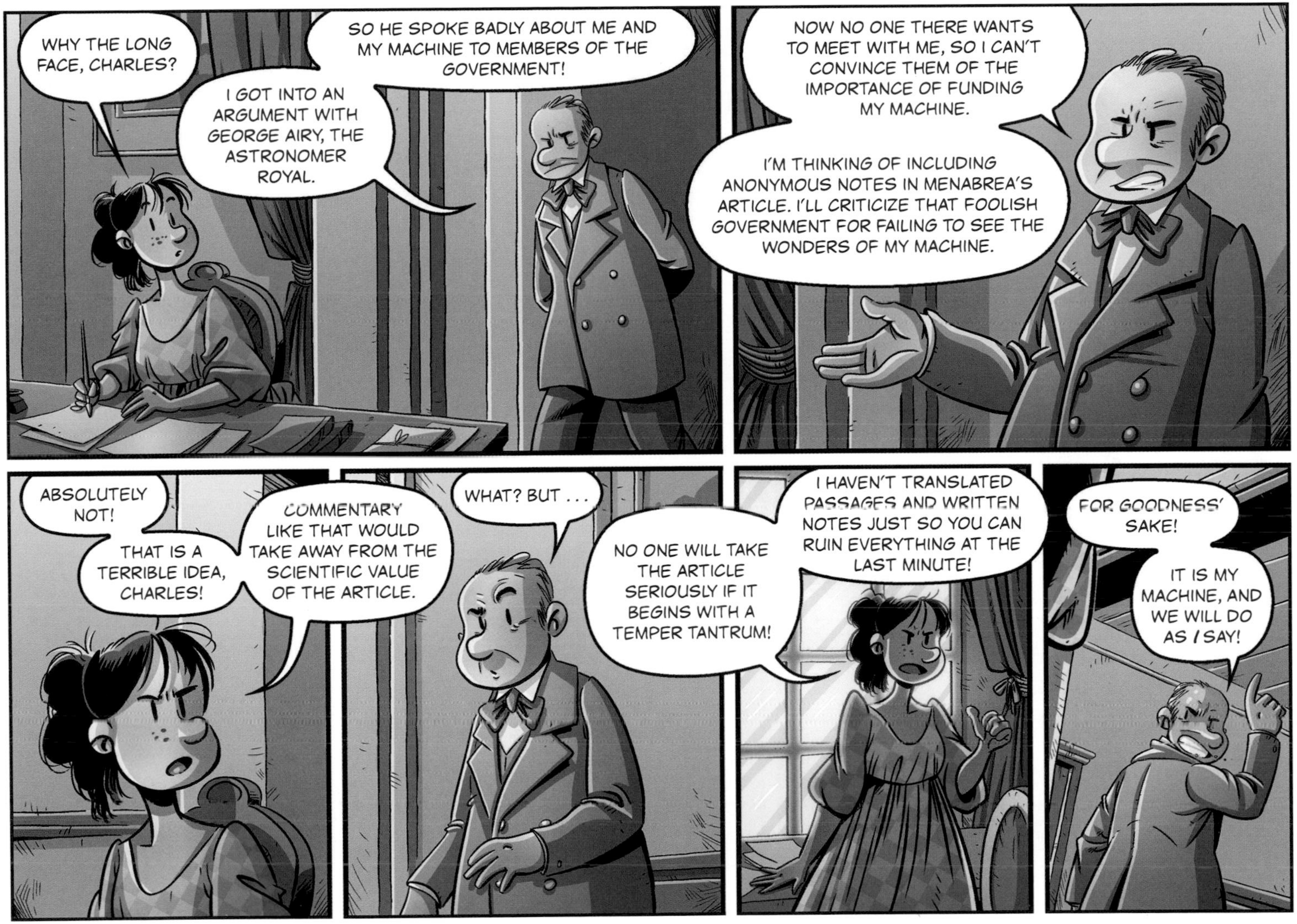
WHY THE LONG FACE, CHARLES?
SO HE SPOKE BADLY ABOUT ME AND MY MACHINE TO MEMBERS OF THE GOVERNMENT!
I GOT INTO AN ARGUMENT WITH GEORGE AIRY, THE ASTRONOMER ROYAL.
NOW NO ONE THERE WANTS TO MEET WITH ME, SO I CAN'T CONVINCE THEM OF THE IMPORTANCE OF FUNDING MY MACHINE.
I'M THINKING OF INCLUDING ANONYMOUS NOTES IN MENABREA'S ARTICLE. I'LL CRITICIZE THAT FOOLISH GOVERNMENT FOR FAILING TO SEE THE WONDERS OF MY MACHINE.
ABSOLUTELY NOT!
THAT IS A TERRIBLE IDEA, CHARLES!
COMMENTARY LIKE THAT WOULD TAKE AWAY FROM THE SCIENTIFIC VALUE OF THE ARTICLE.
WHAT? BUT . . .
NO ONE WILL TAKE THE ARTICLE SERIOUSLY IF IT BEGINS WITH A TEMPER TANTRUM!
I HAVEN'T TRANSLATED PASSAGES AND WRITTEN NOTES JUST SO YOU CAN RUIN EVERYTHING AT THE LAST MINUTE!
FOR GOODNESS' SAKE!
IT IS MY MACHINE, AND WE WILL DO AS *I* SAY!

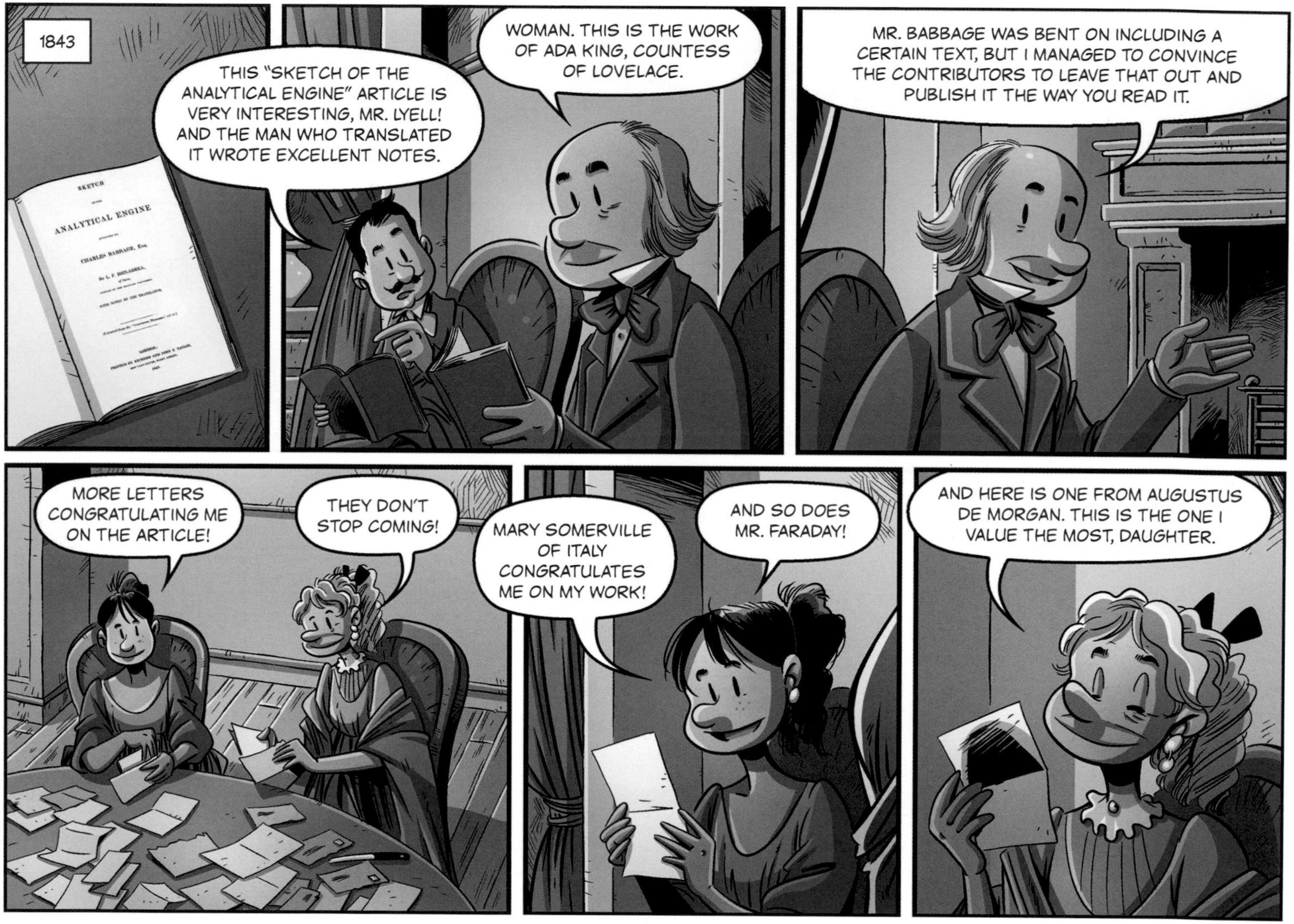
1843
SKETCH
ANALYTICAL ENGINE
THIS "SKETCH OF THE ANALYTICAL ENGINE" ARTICLE IS VERY INTERESTING, MR. LYELL! AND THE MAN WHO TRANSLATED IT WROTE EXCELLENT NOTES.
WOMAN. THIS IS THE WORK OF ADA KING, COUNTESS OF LOVELACE.
MR. BABBAGE WAS BENT ON INCLUDING A CERTAIN TEXT, BUT I MANAGED TO CONVINCE THE CONTRIBUTORS TO LEAVE THAT OUT AND PUBLISH IT THE WAY YOU READ IT.
MORE LETTERS CONGRATULATING ME ON THE ARTICLE!
THEY DON'T STOP COMING!
MARY SOMERVILLE OF ITALY CONGRATULATES ME ON MY WORK!
AND SO DOES MR. FARADAY!
AND HERE IS ONE FROM AUGUSTUS DE MORGAN. THIS IS THE ONE I VALUE THE MOST, DAUGHTER.

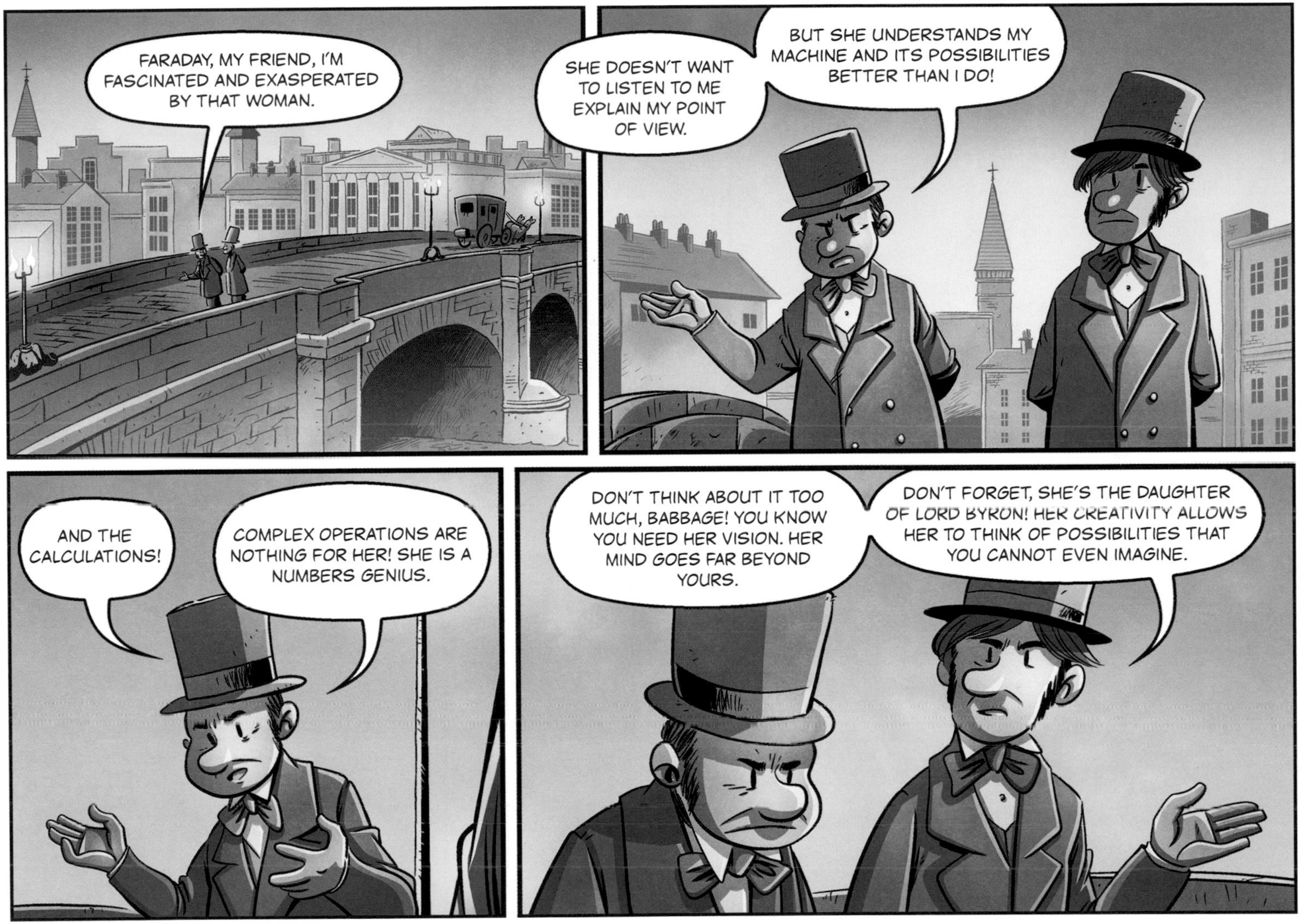
FARADAY, MY FRIEND, I'M FASCINATED AND EXASPERATED BY THAT WOMAN.
SHE DOESN'T WANT TO LISTEN TO ME EXPLAIN MY POINT OF VIEW.
BUT SHE UNDERSTANDS MY MACHINE AND ITS POSSIBILITIES BETTER THAN I DO!
AND THE CALCULATIONS!
COMPLEX OPERATIONS ARE NOTHING FOR HER! SHE IS A NUMBERS GENIUS.
DON'T THINK ABOUT IT TOO MUCH, BABBAGE! YOU KNOW YOU NEED HER VISION. HER MIND GOES FAR BEYOND YOURS.
DON'T FORGET, SHE'S THE DAUGHTER OF LORD BYRON! HER CREATIVITY ALLOWS HER TO THINK OF POSSIBILITIES THAT YOU CANNOT EVEN IMAGINE.

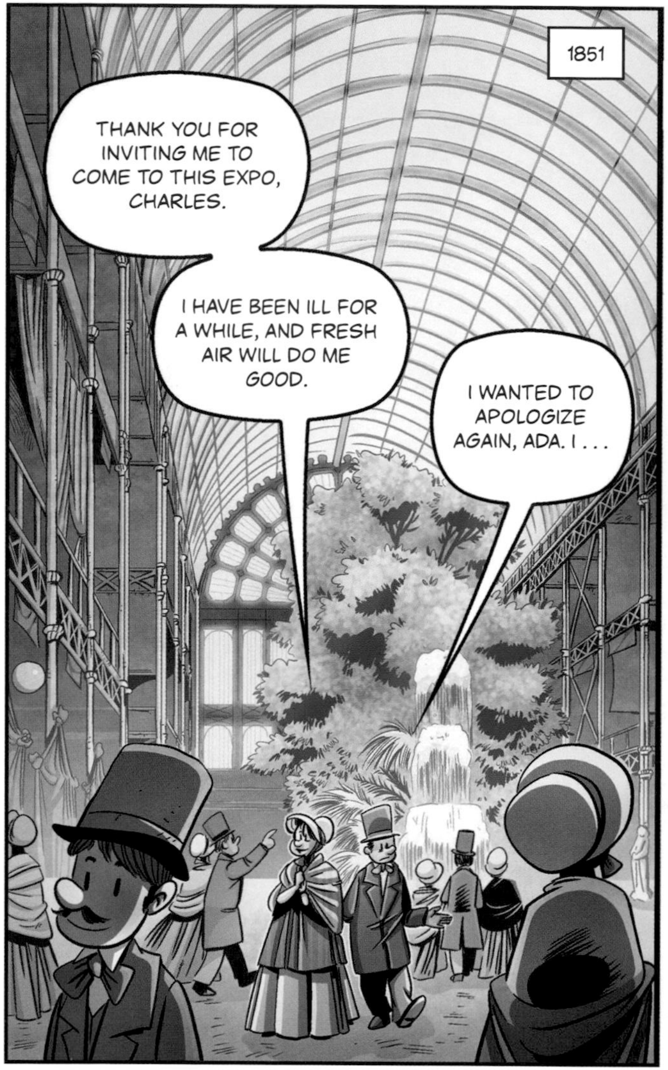
1851
THANK YOU FOR INVITING ME TO COME TO THIS EXPO, CHARLES.
I HAVE BEEN ILL FOR A WHILE, AND FRESH AIR WILL DO ME GOOD.
I WANTED TO APOLOGIZE AGAIN, ADA. I . . .

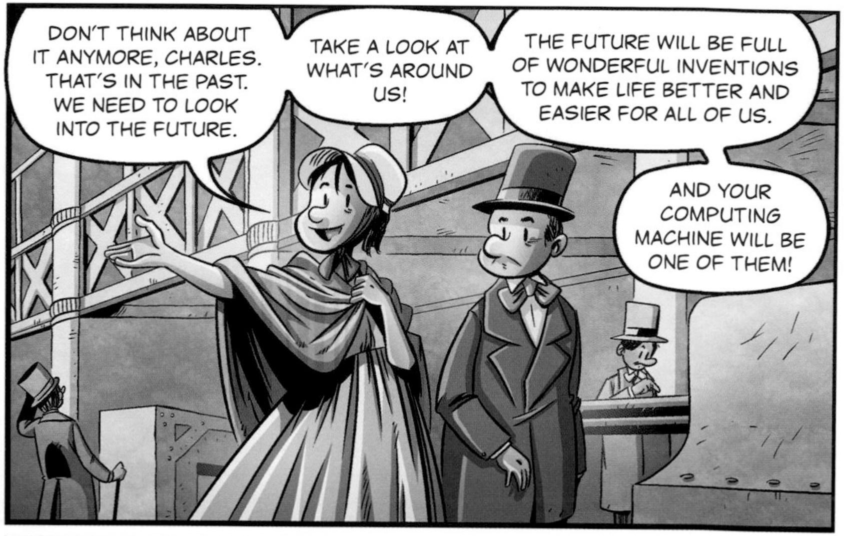
DON'T THINK ABOUT IT ANYMORE, CHARLES. THAT'S IN THE PAST. WE NEED TO LOOK INTO THE FUTURE.
TAKE A LOOK AT WHAT'S AROUND US!
THE FUTURE WILL BE FULL OF WONDERFUL INVENTIONS TO MAKE LIFE BETTER AND EASIER FOR ALL OF US.
AND YOUR COMPUTING MACHINE WILL BE ONE OF THEM!

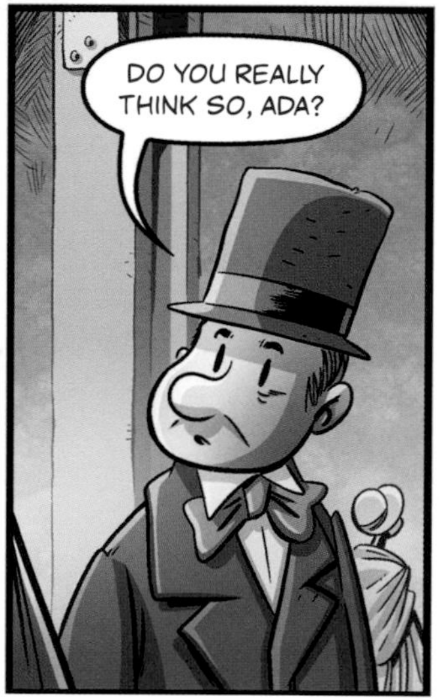
DO YOU REALLY THINK SO, ADA?

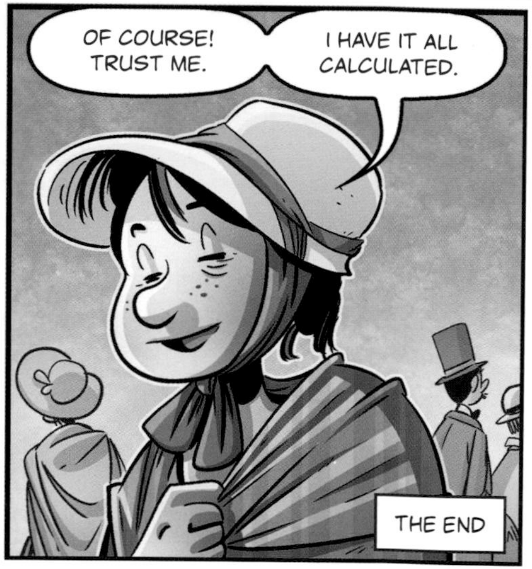
OF COURSE! TRUST ME.
I HAVE IT ALL CALCULATED.
THE END

TIMELINE

1815   Augusta Ada Byron is born in London, England, on December 10.

1828   She applies her childhood education toward creating designs for flying machines.

1833   She meets mathematician Charles Babbage through an introduction from Mary Somerville, and they begin a correspondence.

1835   She marries William King-Noel.

1838   She receives the title *Countess of Lovelace*, with her husband receiving the title *Earl of Lovelace*.

1841   She resumes her studies, this time with mathematician Augustus De Morgan.

1842   She begins to translate an article by mathematician Luigi Menabrea about Babbage's proposed analytical machine, "Sketch of the Analytical Engine Invented by Charles Babbage, Esq."

1843   The translation is published with new notes from Lovelace. Her additions clarify difficult concepts and include the first published computer algorithm.

1852   She dies on November 27 from uterine cancer.

GLOSSARY

ALGEBRAICAL: related to the branch of mathematics known as algebra

ANALYTICAL: involving the mathematical methods of algebra and calculus

ANALYTICAL ENGINE: a mechanical calculator proposed by Charles Babbage and intended for more complex computations than his difference engine could do

AUTOMATA: mechanical devices that move based on programmed responses and that often resemble human figures

AUTOMATED: operating automatically and without human involvement

CALCULUS: an advanced branch of mathematics

CARTOGRAPHY: the study and process of drawing maps

COMPUTATION: a mathematical calculation

DATA: information, often in the form of mathematical figures

DIFFERENCE ENGINE: a mechanical calculator designed by Charles Babbage for polynomial functions

DIFFERENTIAL: a mathematical expression based on the derivative of a function

LOGARITHM TABLE: a chart used to find particular mathematical figures without making calculations

OPERATION: a mathematical process

POLYNOMIAL FUNCTION: a mathematical expression that includes variables and coefficients

ROYAL ASTRONOMICAL SOCIETY: a group founded in 1820 to promote the study of astronomy and the solar system

SEXTANT: an instrument used in navigation to measure distances between objects

TEXTILE: a type of fabric, usually created through weaving

THEOREM: a rule of mathematics, expressed with symbols

FURTHER RESOURCES

"Ada Lovelace: Grandmother of Computing Mini Bio"
    https://youtu.be/InyyT4OiYFY

Bayarri, Jordi. *Mary Anning and the Great Fossil Discoveries*. Minneapolis: Graphic Universe,
    2023.

Bodden, Valerie. *Programming Pioneer Ada Lovelace*. Minneapolis: Lerner Publications, 2017.

"The Greatest Machine That Never Was"
    https://youtu.be/FlfChYGv3Z4

Preuitt, Sheela. *Girl Code Revolution: Profiles and Projects to Inspire Coders*. Minneapolis:
    Lerner Publications, 2021.

INDEX